Trans
HE
4491
.B69
A45
1868

B

MINUTES
COMM'R'S
RAPID
TRANSIT
1888.

Transportation
Library

HE
4491
.B89
A45
1888

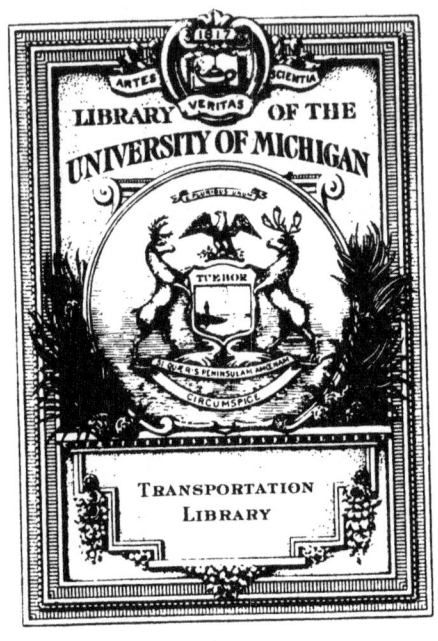

MINUTES

AND

PROCEEDINGS

OF THE

Commissioners of Rapid Transit

APPOINTED BY

Hon. Alfred C. Chapin, Mayor of the City of Brooklyn,

FEBRUARY 4TH, 1888.

BROOKLYN:
BROOKLYN CITIZEN PRINT, 397 TO 403 FULTON STREET.
1888.

CITY OF BROOKLYN,
Thursday, February 16, 1888.

The Commissioners appointed by Hon. Alfred C. Chapin Mayor of the City of Brooklyn, under authority of Chapter 606 of the Laws of 1875, and the Acts amendatory thereof, on the fourth day of February, 1888, viz.: Thomas S. Moore, George W. Almy, George W. Brown, Thomas H. McGrath and Eugene Doherty, met at 9 A. M. this day at Room 6, Hall of Records, all the Commissioners being present.

On motion the following was adopted :

Resolved, That we, the Commissoners appointed by the Hon. Alfred C. Chapin, Mayor of the City of Brooklyn, under authority of Chapter 606, of the Laws of 1875, and the several acts amendatory thereof, on the fourth day of February, 1888, do now organize as a Board by the election of President, Treasurer and Secretary as permanent officers of the Board.

The following officers were unanimously elected.

THOMAS S. MOORE, President.
GEORGE W. ALMY, Treasurer.
GEORGE W. BROWN, Secretary.

On motion it was

Resolved, That all persons employed by this Board shall receive compensation only when money sufficient for that purpose shall have been collected as an assessment upon subscribers to the stock of such Company as may by this Board be organized under Chapter 606 of the Laws of 1875, and all contracts for printing, advertising and supplies shall be made subject to the same condition, and said condition shall be expressly assented to by all persons contracting with this Board.

On motion it was

Resolved, that the following notice be published :

RAPID TRANSIT COMMISSION.

Notice is hereby given that the undersigned Commissioners, appointed by the Mayor of the City of Brooklyn, pursuant to the provisions of Chapter 606 of the Laws of 1875, and acts amending the same, will meet in Room 6, Hall of Records, Fulton Street, Brooklyn, on Monday evening, February 20th, 1888, at eight o'clock, to hear persons who are interested in the matter of the necessity or need of a steam railway wholly within the limits of the City of Brooklyn, commencing at a point or points at or near Greenpoint Ferry, and also points bordering on the Newtown Creek; thence along, and within a distance convenient for such purpose, the line of the East River, to a point at or near the ferries of said river side and at Broadway; thence along Wythe Avenue and along Franklin Avenue to Myrtle Avenue or some other street or avenue adjacent or parallel thereto; and thence by some convenient route to a point at or near the City Hall.

And, also, from the said junction of Franklin and Myrtle Avenues by some convenient and adequate route to and through the southern parts of the said City and from that junction of said avenues and junction of other avenues and streets, to and through other parts of the City as may be necessary and convenient to provide additional routes, or portion of routes, and extensions in other and further directions, as required by public needs.

Dated Brooklyn, February 16, 1888.

THOMAS S. MOORE,
GEORGE W. ALMY,
GEORGE W. BROWN. } *Commissioners.*
THOMAS H. McGRATH,
EUGENE DOHERTY,

On motion it was

Resolved, That the Secretary be directed to notify his Honor, the Mayor, of the fact that this Board has organized by the election of President, Treasurer, and Secretary.

Resolved, that the Board extend to his Honor the invitation to attend such of its meetings as may suit his convenience and pleasure.

A copy of the application made to his Honor the Mayor, by householders and tax payers of the City of Brooklyn, County of Kings, signed and duly verified by Thomas D. Mosscrop and David S. Stewart, was produced, and the Secretary was directed to enter the same upon the minutes of the Board together with the certificate of appointment of the said Commissioners.

The said copy was in the words and figures following:

TO THE MAYOR OF THE CITY OF BROOKLYN:

We, the undersigned, and each of us, a householder and tax payer of the County of Kings, of the State of New York, represent that there is, in our opinion, and in the opinion of each of us, need of a steam elevated railway and railways within the said City of Brooklyn for the transportation therein of passengers from a point or points at or near Greenpoint Ferry, and also points bordering on the Newtown Creek, thence along and within a distance convenient for such purposes, of the line of the East River to a point at or near the ferries on said river side and at Broadway; thence along Wythe Avenue and along Franklin Avenue to Myrtle Avenue or some other street, or avenue, adjacent or parallel thereto; and thence by some convenient route to a point at or near the City Hall, and also, from the said junction of Franklin and Myrtle Avenues by some convenient and adequate route, to and through the southern parts of the said City, and from that junction of said avenues and junctions of other avenues and streets to and through other parts of the City as may be necessary and convenient to provide additional routes or portions of routes, and extensions, in other and further directions, as required by public needs; and the undersigned, your Petitioners, respectfully request the Mayor of the City of Brooklyn to appoint five Commissioners for the purpose of determing upon the necessity of such railway or railways, and for fixing and determining the route and routes thereof, and for such purpose and other purposes in pursuance of and according to the provisions of the Act of the Legislature of the State of New York, passed June 18, 1875, entitled, "An Act to provide for the construction and operation of a steam railway or railways in the Counties of the State," and Acts additional and amendatory thereof.

And your Petitioners will ever pray.

Dated at the City of Brooklyn,
December 23, 1887.

P. J. Kenedy,	130 St. Marks' avenue.
H. C. Wheeler,	966 Kent avenue.
J. M. White,	233 Park place.
George W. Chauncey,	257 Henry street.
I. W. Bon,	217 Clermont avenue.
Cyrus E. Stayles,	113 Remsen street.
Proctor Walter, a. s.,	24 Herkimer street.
John S. Drake,	94 Monroe street.
Alexander Ray,	128 Roger avenue.
J. P. Crawford,	51 Seventh avenue.
Richard B. Leech,	51 Putnam avenue.
John P. Hudson,	1413 Pacific street.
John A. Sharp,	438 Grand avenue.
George S. James,	1088 Fulton street.
Bernard Fowler,	1153 Pacific street.
A. P. Blanchard,	992 Dean street.
Howard M. Smith,	87 Hancock street.
J. B. Davenport,	372 Washington avenue.
William Harkness,	566 Washington avenue.
Wm. S. Carlisle,	405 Classon avenue.

A. Abraham,	63 South Oxford street.
Henry Mumford,	218 Quincy street.
Charles C. Oliver,	231 Monroe street.
Adam H. Leich,	314 Monroe street.
Jas. Gildersleeve,	428 Gold street.
J. H. Benedict,	41 Cambridge place.
Charles Small,	95 South Ninth street.
Geo. H. Palmer,	Glenmore, c. Van Sindern.
William D. Lacy,	354 Dean street.
David S. Arnott,	705 Fourth avenue.
Benjamin W. Wilson,	165 Ross street.
Thomas D. Hudson,	927 Bedford avenue.
J. J. Vail,	245 Jefferson avenue.
Chas. S. Barker,	166 Classon avenue.
N. Cooper,	34 Seventh avenue.
William Berri,	401 Grand avenue.
Thomas B. Rutan.	173 Monroe street.
B. C. Miller,	979 Bergen street.
F. W. Miller,	998 Bergen street.
William Herod,	976 St. Marks' avenue.
James White,	446 Adelphi street.
William H. Taylor,	65 Cambridge place.
John Q. Adams,	871 Union street.
A. H. Daily,	451 Washington avenue.
D. H. Valentine,	120 Kent avenue, E. D.
Thomas D. Mosscrop,	22 Leffert's place.
D. P. Darling,	420 Grand avenue.
William T. Lane,	1389 Pacific street.
Peter Milne,	33 Cambridge place.
R. Lehmen,	81 Montrose avenue.
D. H. Way,	161 Fort Green place
W. Watson,	Hendrix street.
Thomas H. Learey,	217 Lincoln place.

STATE OF NEW YORK, }
  Kings County, } *s.s.:*
  City of Brooklyn. }

Thomas D. Mosscrop, being duly sworn, says: That he resides at 22 Leffert's Place, in the City of Brooklyn; that he has read the foregoing petition signed by him, one of the said petitioners, and also a householder and tax payer; that he knows the contents thereof, and that the same are true to his own knowledge, except as to those matters therein stated on information and belief, and as to those matters he believes them to be true.

THOMAS D. MOSSCROP.

Sworn to before me, this 21st day of December, 1887.
C. E. PRATT,
Justice Supreme Court.

STATE OF NEW YORK, ⎫
   Kings County. ⎬ s.s.:
   City of Brooklyn. ⎭

David S. Stewart, being duly sworn, says: That he resides at No. 53 Putnam Avenue, in the City of Brooklyn; that he was present and saw each of the several persons whose names are signed to the foregoing petition, sign the same; that he knows each and every one of them personally; that each of them is a householder and taxpayer in the City of Brooklyn; that such signatures are genuine; that he has read the foregoing petition and knows the contents thereof, and that the same are true to his own knowledge, except as to those matters therein stated on information and belief, and as to those matters he believes them to be true.

DAVID S. STEWART.

Sworn to before me, this 31st day of December, 1887.
C. E. PRATT,
Justice of Supreme Court.

I hereby certify that the annexed is a true copy of the petition for appointment of Commissioners, under Chapter 606 of the Laws of the State of New York of 1875, presented to his Honor, Mayor Alfred C. Chapin, Brooklyn, January 9, 1888.

DANIEL B. PHILLIPS.

Brooklyn, February 17, 1888.

In the Matter of the Application of
P. J. Kenedy, George W. Chauncey,
Thomas B. Rutan, David Valentine,
George W. Palmer and others,
for the appointment of Commissioners
under and in pursuance of
the provisions of Chapter Six
hundred and six, of the Laws of
1875.

The foregoing application, having within thirty days last past been presented to me duly verified upon oath, before a Justice of the Supreme Court, and appearing to my satisfaction that such application is duly made by fifty reputable householders and tax payers in the City of Brooklyn and County of Kings; and it further appearing by the said application, duly verified as aforesaid, that there is need in the said City of Brooklyn, in the said County of Kings, of a steam railway or steam railways for the transportation of passengers, and that the railway and railways proposed in and by the said application shall be wholly within the limits of the said City of Brooklyn.

I, the undersigned, Alfred C. Chapin, as Mayor of the City of Brooklyn, acting in this matter under and by virtue of the power and authority conferred upon me, and by an Act of the Legislature of the State of New York, passed June 18, 1875, entitled "An act further to provide for the construction and operation of a steam railway or railways in counties of the State," do hereby appoint

    Thomas S. Moore,
    George W. Almy,
    George W. Brown,
    Thomas H. McGrath and
    Eugene Doherty,

(All of whom are residents of the City of Brooklyn, in the County of Kings), as Commissioners, in conformity with the said Act, and with full power and authority in them as such Commissioners to do and provide, and fix and determine all that such Commissioners are in and by the said Act empowered and directed to do and provide.

Witness my hand at the City Hall, in the City of Brooklyn, this fourth day of February, in the year one thousand eight hundred and eighty eight.

The word "January" on the fourteenth line of this page erased, and February inserted instead before execution.

ALFRED C. CHAPIN,
Mayor.

Dan'l B. Phillips,
    Secretary.

A record of the official acts and proceedings of the several Commissioners was read, from which it appeared that a copy of the appointment of each of said Commissioners had been filed in the office of the Secretary of State, and a duplicate thereof had been filed in the office of the Clerk of the County of Kings, within ten days after the appointment of each of said Commissioners, respectively, and that an oath of office, duly made by each of said Commissioners, had within the like period of time been filed in the office of the Secretary of State, a duplicate being in the office of said County Clerk, and that each of said Commissioners had within the like period given a bond as required by said statute, in the penal sum of Twenty-five thousand dollars, with two sufficient surities approved by a Justice of the Supreme Court, which said bonds have been duly filed in the office of the Clerk of said County.

The said oaths and bonds are as follows :

STATE OF NEW YORK, }
  County of Kings, } *ss.:*
  City of Brooklyn, }

In the Matter of the Application of fifty reputable householders and tax payers of the City of Brooklyn, duly verified upon oath before a Justice of the Supreme Court, in and for the County of Kings, for the appointment of Commissioners, under Chapter 606 of the Laws of the State of New York, passed June 18, 1875.

STATE OF NEW YORK, }
  County of Kings, } *ss.:*
  City of Brooklyn, }

I, THOMAS S. MOORE, do solemnly swear that I will support the Constitution of the United States and the Constitution of the State of New York, and that I will faithfully discharge and perform the duties of the office of a Commissioner, under Chapter 606 of the Laws of the State of New York, passed June 18, 1875, and the several acts amendatory thereof, according to the best of my ability.

THOMAS S. MOORE.

Subscribed and sworn to before me, }
  this 13th day of February, 1888. }

EDGAR M. CULLEN,
Justice of the Supreme Court.

(Endorsed.) Filed, February 13, 1888.

A copy.

JOHN M. RANKEN,
Clerk.

STATE OF NEW YORK, } *ss.:*
Office of the Secretary of State. }

I have compared the preceeding with the oath of Thomas S. Moore, filed in this office on the 14th day of February, 1888, and I do hereby certify the same to be a correct transcript therefrom and of the whole thereof.

Witness my hand and Seal of Office of the Secretary of State, at the City of Albany, this 26th day of March, One thousand eight hundred and eighty-eight.

FREDERICK COOK,
Sec'y of State.

Know all men by these presents, that we, Thomas S. Moore, William H. Male, and John W. Frothingham, all of the City of Brooklyn, Kings County and State of New York, are held and firmly bound unto the people of the State of New York in the penal sum of Twenty-five thousand dollars, lawful money of the United States of America, to be paid to the said People of the State of York, for which payment well and truly to be made we bind ourselves, our heirs, executors and administrators, jointly and severally, firmly by these presents.

Sealed with our seals, dated the seventh day of February, One thousand eighth hundred and eighty-eight.

Whereas, the above named Thomas S. Moore has been appointed by the Mayor of the City of Brooklyn, a Commissioner, under and pursuant to the provisions of Chapter 606 of the Laws of the State of New York, passed June 18th, 1875, entitled, "An Act further to provide for the construction and operation of a steam railway or railways in the counties of the State."

Now, therefore, the condition of the above obligation is such that if the above named Thomas S. Moore shall faithfully perform the duties required by him by said Act as such Commissioner, then this obligation to be void, otherwise to remain in full force and virtue.

THOMAS S. MOORE, [L. S.]
W. H. MALE, [L. S.]
JOHN W. FROTHINGHAM, [L. S.]

Sealed and delivered in the presence of

LEWIS W. VAN ANTWERP.

COUNTY OF NEW YORK, } ss.:
City of New York.

WILLIAM H. MALE, one of the sureties named in the within bond, being duly sworn, deposes and says, that he is a resident and householder within the State of New York, and is worth the sum of fifty thousand dollars over all debts and liabilities which he owes or has incurred and exclusive of property exempt by law from levy and sale under execution.

W. H. MALE.

Sworn to before me, this 7th day of February, 1888.

LEWIS W. VAN ANTWERP,
Notary Public,
Kings County.

Certificate filed in N. Y. Co.

COUNTY OF NEW YORK, } ss.:
City of New York,

JOHN W. FROTHINGHAM, one of the sureties named in the within bond, being duly sworn, deposes and says that he is a resident and householder within the State of New York, and is worth the sum of Fifty thousand dollars over all debts and liabilities which he owes or has incurred, and exclusive of property exempt by law from levy and sale under execution.

JOHN W. FROTHINGHAM.

Sworn to before me, this 7th }
day of February, 1888.

LEWIS W. VAN ANTWERP,
Notary Public, Kings County.

Cert. filed in N. Y. County.

COUNTY OF NEW YORK, } ss.:
City of New York.

On this seventh day of February, one thousand eight hundred and eighty-eight, before me personally appeared Thomas S. Moore, William H. Male and John W. Frothingham, all to me known to be the same persons described in and who executed the within instrument, and they severally acknowledged to me that they executed the same.

LEWIS W. VAN ANTWERP,
Notary Public, Kings County.

Cert. filed in N. Y. Co.

STATE OF NEW YORK, } ss.:
County of Kings,

I, JOHN M. RANKEN, Clerk of the County of Kings, and Clerk of the Supreme Court of the State of New York, in and for said County (said Court being a Court of Record), do hereby certify that I have compared the annexed with the original bond filed and recorded in my office, February 10, 1888, and that the same is a true transcript thereof, and of the whole of such original.

In testimony whereof, I have hereunto set my hand and affixed the seal of said County and Court, this 10th day of February, 1888.

JOHN M. RANKEN.

STATE OF NEW YORK, }
  County of Kings,   } ss.:
  City of Brooklyn. }

In the Matter of the Application of fifty reputable householders and tax payers of the City of Brooklyn, duly verified upon oath before a Justice of the Supreme Court, in and for the County of Kings, for the appointment of Commissioners, under Chapter 606 of the Laws of the State of New York, passed June 18, 1875.

STATE OF NEW YORK, }
  County of Kings,   } ss.:
  City of Brooklyn, }

I, GEORGE W. ALMY, do solemnly swear that I will support the Constitution of the United States, and the Constitution of the State of New York, and that I will faithfully discharge the duties of the office of a Commissioner under Chapter 606 of the Laws of the State of New York, passed June 18, 1875, and the several acts amendatory thereof, according to the best of my ability.

GEORGE W. ALMY.

Subscribed and sworn to before me, }
  this 13th day of February, 1888. }

    EDGAR M. CULLEN,
        Justice of the Supreme Court,

(Endorsed.) Filed Feb'y 13, 1888.

        A copy.
                    JOHN M. RANKEN,
                              Clerk.

STATE OF NEW YORK, } ss.:
Office of the Secretary of State. }

I have compared the preceding with the oath of George W. Almy, filed in this office on the 14th day of February, 1888, and I do hereby certify the same to be a correct transcript therefrom and of the whole thereof.

Witness my hand and the seal of office of the Secretary of State, at the City of Albany, this 26th day of March, one thousand eight hundred and eighty-eight.

FREDERICK COOK,
Secretary of State.

Know all men by these presents that we, George W. Almy, John Wygand and William J. La Roche, all of the City of Brooklyn, Kings County, and State of New York, are held and firmly bound unto the people of the State of New York, in the penal sum of Twenty-five thousand dollars, lawful money of the United States of America, to be paid to the said People of the State of New York, for which payment well and truly to be made, we bind ourselves, our heirs, executors and administrators, jointly and severally firmly by these presents.

Sealed with our seals, dated the seventh day of February, one thousand eight hundred and eighty-eight.

Whereas the above named George W. Almy has been appointed by the Mayor of the City of Brooklyn a Commissioner, under and pursuant to the provisions of Chapter 606 of the Laws of the State of New York, passed June 18, 1875, entitled "An act further to provide for the construction and operation of a steam railway or railways in the Counties of the State."

Now, therefore, the condition of the above obligation is such that if the above George W. Almy shall faithfully perform the duties required of him by said Act, as such

Commissioner, then this obligation to be void, otherwise to remain in full force and virtue.

   Signed, GEORGE W. ALMY, [L. S.]
        JOHN WYGAND, [L. S.]
        W. J. LA ROCHE. [L. S.]
Sealed and delivered in the presence of
      F. M. HAVILAND.

NEW YORK COUNTY, } ss.:
City of New York,

JOHN WYGAND, one of the sureties named in the within bond being duly sworn, deposes and says, that he is a resident and householder within the State of New York, and is worth the sum of Fifty thousand dollars over all the debts and liabilities which he owes or has incurred, and exclusive of property exempt by law from levy and sale under execution.

         JOHN WYGAND.

Sworn to before me, this 7th }
day of February, 1888.
   F. M. HAVILAND, [L. S.]
    Notary Public, (201),
     (22 Park Place.)
   City and County of New York.

NEW YORK COUNTY, } ss.:
City of New York,

W. J. LA ROCHE, one of the sureties named in the within bond, being duly sworn, deposes and says, that he is a resident and householder within the State of New York and is worth the sum of Fifty thousand dollars, over all his debts and liabilities which he owes or has incurred, and exclusive of property exempt by law from levy and sale under execution.

        W. J. LA ROCHE.

Sworn to before me, this 7th }
day of February, 1888,
   F. M. HAVILAND, [L. S.]
    Notary Public, (201),
     (22 Park Place.)
   City and County of New York.

NEW YORK COUNTY, } ss.:
City of New York,

On this seventh day of February, one thousand eight hundred and eighty-eight, before me personally appeared George W. Almy, John Wygand, and W. J. La Roche, all to me known to be the same persons described in and who executed the within instrument, and they severally acknowledged to me that they executed the same.

[L. S.]   F. M. HAVILAND,
Notary Public, (201),
(22 Park Place.)
City and County of New York.

STATE OF NEW YORK, } ss.:
City and County of New York.

I, JAMES A. FLACK, Clerk of the City and County of New York, and also Clerk of the Supreme Court for the said City and County, the same being a Court of Record, do hereby certify that M. F. Haviland has filed in the Clerk's office of the County of New York, a certified copy of his appointment as Notary Public for the County of Kings, with his autograph signature, and was, at the time of taking the proof or acknowledgment of the annexed instrument, duly authorized to take the same. And, further, that I am well acquainted with the handwriting of such Notary and verily believe the signature to the said certificate of proof or acknowledgment to be genuine.

In testimony whereof, I have hereunto set my hand and affixed the seal of the said Court and County the 8th day of February, 1888.

JAMES A. FLACK,
Clerk.

STATE OF NEW YORK, } ss.:
County of Kings,

I, JOHN M. RANKEN, Clerk of the County of Kings, and Clerk of the Supreme Court of the State of New York, in and for said County, (said Court being a Court of Record) do hereby certify that I have compared the annexed with the original bond filed and recorded in my office, February 10th, 1888, and that the same is a true transcript thereof, and of the whole of such original.

In testimony whereof, I have hereunto set my hand and affixed the seal of said County and Court, this 10th day of February, 1888.

JOHN M. RANKEN,
Clerk.

STATE OF NEW YORK, }
County of Kings, } ss.:
City of Brooklyn, }

In the Matter of the Application of fifty reputable householders and tax payers of the City of Brooklyn, duly verified upon oath before a Justice of the Supreme Court, in and for the County of Kings, for the appointment of Commissioners, under Chapter 606 of the Laws of the State of New York, passed June 18, 1875.

STATE OF NEW YORK, }
County of Kings, } ss.:
City of Brooklyn, }

I, GEORGE W. BROWN, do solemnly swear, that I will support the Constitution of the United States and the Constitution of the State of New York, and that I will faithfully discharge and perform the duties of the office of a Commissioner under Chapter 606 of the Laws of the State

of New York, passed June 18, 1875, and the several Acts
amendatory thereof, according to the best my ability.
GEORGE W. BROWN.

Subscribed and sworn to before me,
this 13th day of February, 1888.

EDGAR M. CULLEN,
Justice of the Supreme Court.

(Endorsed.) Filed, February 13, 1888.
A copy.
JOHN M. RANKEN,
Clerk.

STATE OF NEW YORK, } ss.:
Office of the Secretary of State,

I have compared the preceding with the oath of George
W. Brown, filed in this office on the 14th day of February,
1888, and I do hereby certify the same to be a correct transcript therefrom, and of the whole thereof.

Witness my hand and the seal of Office of the
Secretary of State at the City of Albany, this 26th
day of March, One thousand eight hundred and
eighty-eight.
FREDERICK COOK.
Secretary of State.

Know all men by these presents that we, George W.
Brown, Samuel Richards and Charles Cooper, all of the
City of Brooklyn, Kings County, and State of New York,
are held and firmly bound unto the people of the State of
New York in the penal sum of Twenty-five thousand dollars, lawful money of the United States of America to be
paid to the said People of the State of New York, for which
payment well and truly to be made we bind ourselves, our
heirs, executors and administrators, jointly and severally
firmly by these presents.

Sealed with our seals, dated the tenth day of February, one thousand eight hundred and eighty-eight.

Whereas the above named George W. Brown has been appointed by the Mayor of the City of Brooklyn, a Commissioner, under and pursuant to the provisions of Chapter 606 of the Laws of the State of New York, passed June 18, 1875, entitled "An act further to provide for the construction and operation of a steam railway or railways in the counties of the State."

Now, therefore, the condition of the said obligation is such that if the above named George W. Brown shall faithfully perform the duties required of him by said Act as such Commissioner, then this obligation to be void, otherwise to remain in full force and virtue.

GEORGE W. BROWN, [L. S.]
SAMUEL RICHARDS, [L. S.]
CHARLES COOPER, [L. S.]

Sealed and delivered in the presence of
J. M. MILLS.

KINGS COUNTY, } ss:
City of Brooklyn.

SAMUEL RICHARDS, one of the sureties named in the within bond, being duly sworn, deposes and says that he is a resident and householder within the State of New York, and is worth the sum of Twenty-five thousand-dollars over all the debts and liabilities which he owes or has incurred, and exclusive of property exempt by law from levy and sale under execution.

SAMUEL RICHARDS.

Sworn to before me this }
10th day of February, 1888.

J. M. MILLS,
Notary Public,
Kings County.

KINGS COUNTY, } ss:
City of Brooklyn.

CHARLES COOPER, one of the sureties named in the within bond, being duly sworn, deposes and says that he is a resident and householder within the State of New York, and is worth the sum of Twenty-five thousand dollars over all the debts and liabilities which he owes or has incurred, and exclusive of property exempt by law from levy and sale under execution.

CHARLES COOPER.

Sworn to before me this }
10th day of February, 1888.

J. M. MILLS,
Notary Public,
Kings County.

KINGS COUNTY, } ss:
City of Brooklyn.

On this tenth day of February, one thousand eight hundred and eighty-eight, before me personally appeared George W. Brown, Samuel Richards and Charles Cooper, all to me known to be the same persons described in and who executed the within instrument, and they severally acknowledged to me that they executed the same.

J. M. MILLS,
Notary Public,
Kings County.

STATE OF NEW YORK, } ss.:
County of Kings.

I, JOHN M. RANKEN, Clerk of the County of Kings, and Clerk of the Supreme Court of the State of New York, in and for said County (said Court being a Court of Record), do hereby certify that I have compared the annexed with the original bond filed and recorded in my office, February 13, 1888, and that the same is a true transcript thereof, and of the whole of such original.

In testimony whereof, I have hereunto set my hand and affixed the seal of said County and Court, this 13th day of February, 1888.

JOHN M. RANKEN,

Clerk.

STATE OF NEW YORK,)
County of Kings. } *ss.:*
City of Brooklyn,)

In the Matter of the Application of fifty reputable householders and tax payers of the City of Brooklyn, duly verified upon oath before a Justice of the Supreme Court, in and for the County of Kings, for for the appointment of Commissioners under Chapter 606 of the Laws of the State of New York, passed June 18, 1875.

STATE OF NEW YORK,)
County of Kings, } *ss.:*
City of Brooklyn.)

I, THOMAS H. MCGRATH, do solemnly swear that I will support the Constitution of the United States and the Constitution of the State of New York, and that I will faithfully discharge and perform the duties of the office of a Commissioner, under Chapter 606 of the Laws of the

State of New York, passed June 18, 1875, and the several acts amendatory thereof, to the best of my ability.

THOMAS H. McGRATH.

Subscribed and sworn to before me, } this 13th day of February, 1888. }

EDGAR M. CULLEN,
Justice of the Supreme Court.
(Endorsed.) Filed February 13, 1888.
A copy.
JOHN M. RANKEN,
Clerk.

STATE OF NEW YORK, } ss.:
Office of the Secretary of State, }

I have compared the preceding with the oath of Thomas H. McGrath, filed in this office on the 14th day of February, 1888, and I do hereby certify the same to be a correct transcript therefrom and of the whole thereof.

Witness my hand and seal of office of the Secretary of State, at the City of Albany, this 26th day of March, one thousand eight hundred and eighty eight.

FREDERICK COOK,
Secretary of State.

Known all men by these presents, that we, Thomas H. McGrath, Alanson Tredwell and Hermanus B. Hubbard, all of the City of Brooklyn, Kings County and State of New York, are held and firmly bound unto the people of the State of New York in the penal sum of Twenty-five thousand dollars lawful money of the United States of America, to be paid to the said people of the State of New York, for which payment well and truly to be made, we bind ourselves, our heirs, executors and administrators, jointly and severally, firmly by these presents.

Sealed with our seals, dated the eighth day of February, One thousand eight hundred and eighty-eight.

Whereas, the above named Thomas H. McGrath has been appointed by the Mayor of the City of Brooklyn a Commissioner, under and pursuant to the provisions of Chapter 606 of the Laws of the State of New York, passed June 18th, 1875, entitled "An Act further to provide for the construction and operation of a steam railway or railways in the counties of the State."

Now, therefore, the condition of the above obligation is such that if the above named Thomas H. McGrath shall faithfully perform the duties required of him by said act, as such Commissioner, then this obligation to be void, otherwise to remain in full force and virtue.

THOMAS H. McGRATH, [L. S.]
ALANSON TREDWELL, [L. S.]
H. B. HUBBARD, [L. S.]

Sealed and delivered in the presence of
REMSEN DIKEMAN.

KINGS COUNTY, } ss.:
City of Brooklyn, }

ALANSON TREDWELL, one of the sureties named in the within bond, being duly sworn, deposes and says, that he is a resident and householder within the State of New York and is worth the sum of Fifty thousand dollars over all the debts and liabilities which he owes or has incurred, and exclusive of property exempt by law from levy and sale under execution.

ALANSON TREDWELL.

Sworn to before me, this 8th }
day of February, 1888. }

REMSEN DIKEMAN,
Notary Public,
Kings County, N. Y.

KINGS COUNTY } ss.:
City of Brooklyn,

HERMANUS B. HUBBARD, one of the sureties named in the within bond, being duly sworn deposes and says, that he is a resident and householder within the State of New York, and is worth the sum of fifty thousand dollars over all the debts and liabilities which he owes or has incurred and exclusive of property exempt by law from levy and sale under execution.

H. B. HUBBARD.

Sworn to before me, this 8th }
day of February, 1888.

REMSEN DIKEMAN,
Notary Public,
Kings County, N. Y.

KINGS COUNTY, } ss.:
City of Brooklyn,

On this eighth day of February, One thousand eight hundred and eighty-eight, before me personally appeared Thomas H. McGrath, Alanson Tredwell and Hermanus B. Hubbard all to me known to be the same persons described in and who executed the within instrument, and they severally acknowledged to me that they executed the same

REMSEN DIKEMAN,
Notary Public,
Kings Co., N. Y.

STATE OF NEW YORK, } ss.:
County of Kings,

I, JOHN M. RANKEN, Clerk of the County of Kings and Clerk of the Supreme Court of the State of New York, in and for said County (said Court being a Court of Record) do hereby certify that I have compared the annexed with the original bond filed and recorded in my office February 10, 1888, and that the same is a true transcript thereof, and of the whole of such original.

In testimony whereof I have hereunto set my hand and affixed the seal of said County and Court, this 10th day of February, 1888.

JOHN M. RANKEN,
Clerk.

STATE OF NEW YORK, }
County of Kings, } ss.:
City of Brooklyn. }

In the Matter of the Application of fifty reputable householders and tax payers of the City of Brooklyn, duly verified upon oath before a Justice of the Supreme Court, in and for the County of Kings, for the appointment of Commissioners, under Chapter 606 of the Laws of the State of New York, passed June 18, 1875.

STATE OF NEW YORK, }
County of Kings, } ss.:
City of Brooklyn, }

I, EUGENE DOHERTY, do solemnly swear that I will support the Constitution of the United States and the Constitution of the State of New York, and that I will faithfully discharge and perform the duties of the office of a Commissioner under Chapter 606 of the Laws of the State of New York, passed June 18, 1875, and the several acts amendatory thereof, according to the best of my ability.

EUGENE DOHERTY,

Subscribed and sworn to before me, }
this 13th day of February, 1888. }
EDGAR M. CULLEN,
Justice of the Supreme Court.

(Endorsed.) Filed February 13, 1888.
A copy.

JOHN M. RANKEN,
Clerk.

STATE OF NEW YORK,
Office of the Secretary of State.

I have compared the preceding with the oath of Eugene Doherty, filed in this office on the 14th day of February, 1888, and I do hereby certify the same to be a correct transcript therefrom and of the whole thereof.

Witness my hand and the seal of office of the Secretary of State, at the City of Albany, this 26th day of March, one thousand eight hundred and eighty-eight

FREDERICK COOK,
Secretary of State.

Know all men by these presents that we, Eugene Doherty, Charles Kelbe and Michael O'Keefe, all of the City of Brooklyn, Kings County and State of New York, are held and firmly bound unto the People of the State of New York, in the penal sum of Twenty-five thousand dollars lawful money of the United States of America, to be paid to the said People of the State of New York, for which payment well and truly to be made we bind ourselves, our heirs, executors and administrators, jointly and severally, firmly by these presents.

Sealed with our seals, dated the tenth day of February, one thousand eight hundred and eighty-eight.

Whereas, the above named Eugene Doherty, has been appointed by the Mayor of the City of Brooklyn a Commissioner, under and pursuant to the provisions of Chapter 606 of the Laws of the State of New York, passed June 18th, 1875, entitled "An Act further to provide for the construction and operation of a steam railway or railways in the counties of the State."

Now, therefore, the condition of the above obligation is

such, that if the above-named Eugene Doherty shall faithfully perform the duties required of him by said Act as such Commissioner, then this obligation to be void, otherwise to remain in full force and virtue.

EUGENE DOHERTY, [L. S.]
CHARLES KELBE, [L. S.]
MICHAEL O'KEEFE. [L. S.]

Sealed and delivered in the presence of
JOHN F. CLARK.

KINGS COUNTY, } ss.:
City of Brooklyn,

CHARLES KELBE, one of the sureties named in the within bond, being duly sworn, deposes and says, that he is a resident and householder within the State of New York, and is worth the sum of Twenty-five thousand dollars, over all the debts and liabilities which he owes or has incurred, and exclusive of property exempt by law from levy and sale under execution.

CHARLES KELBE.

Sworn to before me, this 10th day of February, 1888.

J. M. MILLS,
Notary Public,
Kings County.

KINGS COUNTY, } ss.:
City of Brooklyn,

MICHAEL O'KEEFE, one of the sureties named in the within bond, being duly sworn, deposes and says, that he is a resident and householder within the State of New York, and is worth the sum of Twenty-five thousand dollars, over all the debts and liabilities which he owes or has incurred, and exclusive of property exempt by law from levy and sale under execution.

MICHAEL O'KEEFE.

Sworn to before me, this 10th day of February, 1888.

C. F. BROWN,
Justice Supreme Court.

KINGS COUNTY, }
City of Brooklyn; } *ss.:*

On this tenth day of February, one thousand eight hundred and eighty-eight, before me personally appeared Eugene Doherty, Charles Kelbe and Michael O'Keefe, all to me known to be the same persons described in and who executed the within instrument, and they severally acknowledged to me that they executed the same.

J. M MILLS,
Notary Public,
Kings County.

STATE OF NEW YORK, }
County of Kings. }

I, JOHN M. RANKEN, Clerk of the County of Kings, and Clerk of the Supreme Court of the State of New York, in and for said County (said Court being a Court of Record) do hereby certify that I have compared the annexed with the original bond filed and recorded in my office, Feb. 13, 1888, and that the same is a true transcript thereof, and of the whole of such original.

In testimony whereof, I have hereunto set my hand and affixed the seal of said County and Court, this 13th day of February, 1888.

JOHN M. RANKEN,
Clerk.

Adjourned to Friday, Feb. 17, 1888.

CITY OF BROOKLYN,
Friday, Feb. 17, 1888.

The Rapid Transit Commission met pursuant to adjournment.

Present—All the Commissioners.

Minutes of the last meeting read and approved.

The Secretary reported that he had published the notice as directed by the Board three times in the Brooklyn *Eagle*, Brooklyn *Times*, *Standard-Union*, *Citizen* and *Frie Presse*, and that the application for publication in each of these papers was accompanied by a copy of the following letter:—

COMMISSIONERS OF RAPID TRANSIT,
Room No. 6, Hall of Records,
Brooklyn, Feb. 16, 1888.

Dear Sir:

Your attention is called to the following resolution passed by this Board. All work for this Board must comply with it:

Resolved, That all persons employed by this Board shall receive compensation only when money sufficient for that purpose shall have been collected as an assessment upon subscribers to such Company as by this Board may be organized under Chap. 606 of the Laws of 1875, and all the contracts for printing, advertising and supplies shall be made subject to the same condition, and said condition shall be expressly assented to by all persons contracting with this Board.

Please acknowledge in writing your compliance therewith, if agreeable to you.

GEORGE W. BROWN,
Secretary.

The Secretary also reported that he had notified the

Mayor of the organization of the Board by letter of which the following is a copy:

OFFICE OF THE COMMISSIONERS OF RAPID TRANSIT.
Room 6, Hall of Records,
Brooklyn, Feb. 17th, 1888.

HON. ALFRED C. CHAPIN,
Mayor of Brooklyn.

Sir:

I am directed by the Board of Rapid Transit Commissioners, appointed on the 4th inst., to notify you that the said Commissioners have filed their bonds and oaths required by law, and have organized as a Board by the election of President, Treasurer and Secretary.

The Board has the honor to extend to you the invitation to attend such of its meetings as may suit your convenience and pleasure.

Very respectfully,
GEORGE W. BROWN,
Secretary.

There was a general discussion on matters of interest to the Board.

On motion it was voted to accept the offer of Register Murtha of the use of No. Room 6, Hall of Records, as the office of the Commission.

On motion, adjourned to February 20th, at 8 P. M.

GEORGE W. BROWN,
Secretary.

CITY OF BROOKLYN,
Monday, February 20, 1888.

The Board met at 8 o'clock pursuant to adjournment.

Present—All the Commissioners.

The reading of the minutes was dispensed with.

Mr. John W. Locke of South Ninth Street and Wythe enue appeared before the Board and stated that he sired to protest against an Elevated road going through ythe avenue.

Mr. George I. Murphy appeared before the Board and ted that he represented citizens of the 7th, 9th and 24th ards, who desired Rapid Transit connection for those ards with City Hall.

He was requested to present his views in writing at the xt meeting.

Hon. John Winslow appeared before the Board stating at if certain routes were adopted he should desire to pear and oppose them.

Mr. Hoff of Nostrand avenue stated that he was a operty owner there and desired at a proper time to oppose elevated railroad through that avenue.

On motion it was voted to employ an assistant secretary o should be a stenographer, under the conditions of the olution passed February 16th.

The names of Mr. William Walton and Mrs. Emma F. ttengill were proposed.

On motion the chairman was authorized to engage Mrs. ttengill.

On motion adjourned to Friday evening, February 24th, 8 o'clock.

GEORGE W. BROWN,
Secretary.

COMMISSIONERS OF RAPID TRANSIT,

City of Brooklyn,

Surrogate's Court Room.

February, 24th, 1888.

The Board met pursuant to adjournment.

Present, all the Commissioners.

The reading of the minutes was dispensed with.

George I. Murphy presented some further arguments advocating rapid transit connection from the River Wards to the vicinity of Prospect Park.

Mr. John H. Hoff spoke briefly against the necessity for any rapid transit in that part of the city.

A protest against an Elevated Railroad on Wythe Avenue signed by John B. Hamilton, was received and placed on file.

On motion adjourned to Monday, February 27th, at 4.30 P. M.

GEORGE W. BROWN,
Secretary.

CITY OF BROOKLYN,
February 27, 1888.

Rapid Transit Commission met at Room 6, Hall of Records, at 4.30 P. M., pursuant to adjournment.

Present—All the Commissioners.

The reading of the minutes was dispensed with.

Upon motion by Commissioner Brown, duly seconded, the following resolution was adopted:

Resolved, That these Commissioners hereby determine that there is a necessity in the City of Brooklyn for a steam railway or railways for the transportation of passengers, mails or freight, in addition to any heretofore authorized.

Upon motion duly seconded, it was resolved, that the different Rapid Transit companies now in existence in the City of Brooklyn, be notified that they will be heard in executive session on the subject of routes.

That the Secretary be directed to notify the President of Kings County Railroad, that this Commission will give that company such a hearing in Executive Session on Friday, March 2, 1888, at 9.30 A. M.

That the Secretary be directed to notify the President of the Union and Brooklyn Elevated Railroad Companies, that this Commission will give those companies a hearing on Saturday, March 3, 1888, at 9.30 A. M.

That the Secretary be directed to notify the President of the Long Island Railroad, that this Commission will give that company a hearing on Monday, March 5, 1888, at 9.30 A. M.

On motion, the Commission adjourned to Friday, March 2, 1888, at 9.30 A. M.

GEORGE W. BROWN,
Secretary.

COMMISSIONERS OF RAPID TRANSIT,
City of Brooklyn.
Room No. 6, Hall of Records.
Friday, March 2, 1888, 9.30 A. M.

The Board met pursuant to adjournment.

Present—Commissioners Thomas S. Moore, George W. Almy, George W. Brown, Thomas McGrath and Eugene Doherty.

The reading of the minutes was dispensed with.

There was general discussion as to the matter of routes.

Gen. Jourdan, accompanied by Mr. Chauncey, appeared before the Commission, and presented his views as to desirable routes, and routes which the Kings County Elevated Railroad Company were ready to build.

A petition from owners and representatives of property in the City of Brooklyn, lying south of Atlantic avenue, representing to the Commission the need of Rapid Transit to the southern part of Brooklyn, and in the vicinity of the shore line, was received and placed on file.

A petition from residents and property owners. petitioning the Commission to consider the propriety of laying out elevated railroad connections to enable the people residing east of Washington avenue to reach the South and Wall street ferries, by way of the Fulton Avenue Railroad, by the payment of not more than a single fare for a continuous passage, was also received and placed on file.

On motion the Commission adjourned to Saturday, March 3d, 1888, at 9.30 A. M.. at the Hall of Records.

GEORGE W. BROWN,
Secretary.

COMMISSIONERS OF RAPID TRANSIT,
City of Brooklyn,
Room No. 6, Hall of Records,
Saturday, March 3, 1888, 9 30 A. M.

The Board met pursuant to adjournment.

Present—Commissioners Thomas S. Moore, George W. Almy, George W. Brown, Thomas H. McGrath and Eugene Doherty.

The minutes of the meetings of February 17th, 20th 24th and 27th, and March 2d, were read and approved.

No one appearing on behalf of the Union and Brooklyn Elevated Railroads the meeting adjourned to

Monday, March 5th, 1888, at 9.30 A. M.

GEORGE W. BROWN,
Secretary.

COMMISSIONERS OF RAPID TRANSIT,
City of Brooklyn,
Room No. 6, Hall of Records,
March 5, 9.30 A. M.

The Board met pursuant to adjournment.

Present—Commissioners George W. Almy, George W Brown, Thomas McGrath and Eugene Doherty.

In the absence of Commissioner Moore, Mr. Almy was elected chairman pro tem.

The reading of the minutes of the last meeting was dispensed with.

Mr. W. H. Maxwell, representing the Long Island Elevated Railroad, accompanied by Anthony Jones, the chief engineer of that road appeared before the Commission and stated that the Long Island Elevated Railroad had but one thing to ask of the Commission, namely, that any route which the Commission might lay out to cross the Long Island Elevated Railroad might cross above their proposed structure.

Adjourned tc Wednesday, March 7, 1888, at 4.30 P. M.

GEORGE W. BROWN,
Secretary.

COMMISSIONERS OF RAPID TRANSIT,
City of Brooklyn,
Room No. 6, Hall of Records.
Wednesday, March 7, 1888.

The Board met pursuant to adjournment.

Present—Commissioners Thomas S. Moore, George W. Almy, George W. Brown and Eugene Doherty.

The reading of the minutes was dispensed with.

Hon. John J. Allen appeared before the Commission on behalf of the Fort Hamilton Avenue Elevated Railroad from Fort Hamilton to South Ferry over Third avenue and Atlantic avenue and discussed that route with the Commission.

Resolved, that the Secretary notify the attorneys and Secretary of the Brooklyn Elevated Railroad that this Commission will meet Thursday, March 8th, at 4.30 P. M.

Letters from Mr. Cole, Felix Campbell and Judge Shea were received and placed on file.

On motion the Board adjourned to Thursday, March 8, at 4.30 P. M.

GEORGE W. BROWN,
Secretary.

COMMISSIONERS OF RAPID TRANSIT,
City of Brooklyn,
Room No. 6, Hall of Records,
Thursday, March 8, 1888, 4.30 P. M.

The Board met pursuant to adjournment.

Present—Commissioners Thomas S. Moore, George W. Almy, George W. Brown and Eugene Doherty.

The reading of the minutes of the 3d, 5th and 7th insts. read and approved.

Mr. B. D. Washburn representing Hoadley, Lauterbach & Johnson, attorneys for the Brooklyn and Union Elevated Railroads appeared before the Commission to make inquiries as to what routes had been proposed, and stated that a representative of these companies would meet the Commission at their next meeting.

A petition from residents in the 26th Ward asking for elevated railroad connections from that Ward to South, Wall St. and Fulton Ferries, Bridge, City Hall, etc., was received and placed on file.

On motion, adjourned to Saturday, March 10, 1888, at 9.30 A. M.

GEORGE W. BROWN,
Secretary.

COMMISSIONERS OF RAPID TRANSIT,
City of Brooklyn,
Rooms No. 6, Hall of Records,
Saturday March 10, 1888, 9.30 A M.

The Board met pursuant to adjournment.

Present—Commissioners Thomas S. Moore, George W. Almy, George W. Brown, Thomas H. McGrath and Eugene Doherty.

The reading of the minutes was dispensed with.

Mr. Cohen, representing Messrs. Hoadley, Lauterbach & Johnson, appeared before the Board and stated what parts of the routes already proposed to the Commission the Union Elevated Railroad, and the Brooklyn Elevated Railroad objected to, and the reasons for such objections.

There was general discussion as to routes and other matters of interest to the Commission.

On motion, adjourned to Monday, March 12, 1888, at 4.30 P. M.

GEORGE W. BROWN,
Secretary.

COMMISSIONERS OF RAPID TRANSIT,
City of Brooklyn,
Room No. 6, Hall of Records,
Monday, March 12th, 1888, 4.30 P. M

The Board met pursuant to adjournment.

There being no quorum present the meeting adjourned.

GEORGE W. BROWN,
Secretary.

COMMISSIONERS OF RAPID TRANSIT,
City of Brooklyn,
Room No. 6, Hall of Records,
Saturday, March 17, 1888, 9.30 A. M.

The Board met pursuant to notification by the Secretary.

Present—Commissioners Thomas S. Moore, George W. Almy, George W. Brown, Thomas H. McGrath and Eugene Doherty.

The reading of the minutes was dispensed with.

Petitions from residents and property owners, asking for rapid transit communication from the 13th, 14th and 17th Wards of the City to the City line near Prospect Park, and also South, Wall street, Fulton Ferries and Bridge to the same place, and also from the 9th and 24th Wards to connect with Kings County Elevated Railroad on Fulton avenue, were received and placed on file.

On motion of Commissioner Brown, it was voted to proceed to the nomination of an Engineer for the Board.

Commissioner Brown nominated Samuel R. Probasco.

Commissioner Almy nominated John Y. Culyer.

On motion of Commissioner Almy, action upon these nominations was deferred until the next meeting.

General Jourdan appeared before the Commission by request, and a discussion as to routes was held at some length.

On motion adjourned to March 19th, at 5 P. M.

GEORGE W. BROWN,
Secretary.

COMMISSIONERS OF RAPID TRANSIT,
City of Brooklyn,
Room No. 6, Hall of Records,
Monday, March 19th, 1888.

The Board met pursuant to adjournment.

Present—Commissioners George W. Almy, George W. Brown, Thomas H. McGrath and Eugene Doherty.

Commissioner Almy was elected temporary chairman.

The minutes of the meetings of the 8th, 10th and 12th and 17th insts. were read and approved.

On motion of Commissioner Brown, a notice of a public meeting, to be held on Friday evening next, was ordered to be printed Wednesday, Thursday and Friday, in the *Eagle*, *Standard-Union*, *New York World*, *Citizen*, *Brooklyn Times* and *Frie Presse*, and also to be spread upon the minutes.

The notice was in the following words and figures :

RAPID TRANSIT COMMISSION.

"The undersigned Commissioners, appointed by his Honor, the Mayor of the City of Brooklyn, pursuant to the provisions of Chapter 606 of the Laws of 1875, and the acts amending the same, will meet in the Court Room of the Surrogate's Court, Hall of Records, Fulton street, Brooklyn, on Friday evening, March 23d, 1888, at 8 o'clock, to hear persons who are interested in the matter of the routes of the railways to be located by the said Commission in the City of Brooklyn.

The following routes have been suggested :

The first route begins at the foot of Manhattan avenue ; thence runs to Commercial street; thence through Commercial street to Franklin ; thence through Franklin to

Kent avenue; thence through Kent avenue to Flushing avenue; thence to Nostrand; thence through Nostrand to Bergen street, connecting at Nostrand avenue with the Union Elevated Railway for City Hall; thence through Bergen to the Brighton Beach Railroad west of Franklin.

Or, as an alternative, after coming up Kent avenue, through Classon to Flushing; thence through Flushing to Waverly avenue; thence through Waverly avenue to Atlantic, connecting at Myrtle with the Union Elevated Railroad, and at Fulton avenue with Kings County Elevated Railroad for the City Hall; thence across private property to and across Underhill and Washington venues; thence through Pacific street, or through Washington Avenue and Bergen street to the Brighton Beach Railroad Station.

The second route to begin on Fulton avenue at Sackman street through Fulton avenue to East New York avenue; thence through William or Alabama avenue, to the City Line.

The third route to begin at the junction of Fulton avenue and Joralemon street, through Joralemon to Court street, through Court to Atlantic avenue, through Atlantic avenue or some parallel street to Furman street, through Furman street to Montague street bridge.

The fourth route to begin at the foot of Atlantic avenue and run to Third avenue; thence through Third avenue to the City Line."

On motion, adjourned to Tuesday, March 20th, 1888, at 5 P. M.

GEORGE W. BROWN,
Secretary.

Commissioners of Rapid Transit,

City of Brooklyn,

Room No. 6, Hall of Records,

Tuesday, March 20, 1888, 5 P. M.

The Board met pursuant to adjournment.

Present—Commissioners Thomas S. Moore, George W. Almy, George W. Brown, Thomas H. McGrath and Eugene Doherty.

The minutes of the last meeting read and approved.

On motion of Commissioner Brown it was voted to proceed to the election of an Engineer.

On motion of Commissioner Almy it was voted that the Secretary call the roll, and each Commissioner announce his candidate. Samuel R. Probasco and John Y. Culyer were the only nominees, and a majority of the Board having declared their vote for Mr. Probasco, on motion of Commissioner Almy it was voted that he be declared the Engineer of the Board, subject to the conditions of the resolution relative to incurring of expenses passed February 16th.

The Secretary was ordered to notify Mr. Samuel Probasco of his election as such engineer.

On motion, adjourned to Wednesday, March 21st, at 4.30 P. M.

GEORGE W. BROWN,
Secretary.

Commissioners of Rapid Transit,
City of Brooklyn,
Room No. 6, Hall of Records,
Wednesday, March 21, 1888, 4.30 p.m.

The Board met pursuant to adjournment.

Present—Commissioners Thomas S. Moore, George W. Brown, Thomas H. McGrath and Eugene Doherty and the Engineer of the Board, Mr. Probasco.

The reading of the minutes was dispensed with.

Commissioner Brown stated that he had notified Mr. Probasco of his election as Engineer of the Board, and read Mr. Probasco's acceptance of the appointment. This communication was placed on file.

After informal talk and consultation on matters of interest between Commissioners and Engineer, the meeting adjourned to Friday, evening, March 23, at 8 o'clock.

GEORGE W. BROWN,
Secretary.

Commissioners of Rapid Transit,
City of Brooklyn,
Surrogate's Court Room, Hall of Records,
Friday, March 23, 1888, 8 o'clock p. m.

The Board met pursuant to adjournment to hear persons interested in the proposed routes.

Present—Commissioners Thomas S. Moore, George W.

Almy, George W. Brown, Thomas H. McGrath and Eugene Doherty.

The reading of the minutes was dispensed with.

About one hundred and fifty gentlemen were present.

Mr. Maxwell, representing the Long Island Railroad and the Long Island Elevated Railway, objected to any structure crossing Atlantic avenue at the grade of any present or proposed structure.

Nelson G. Gates, Gen. George Wingate, Dr. Jarrett, George F. Martens, Henry Cook, John Whitten, Noah Tebbets, James Prior, C. F. Beatty, F. R. Moore, Mr. Clark, John Hoff, Mr. Bixedon, Wm. H. Wohlers, F. J. Buckenberger, Jere Johnson, Henry Dosher, F. H. Cowperthwait, residents and property owners on Nostrand avenue protested against a route being laid out through that avenue.

Mr. John Winslow on behalf of property owners on Clinton avenue and Washington avenue, and Messrs, George Nichols, John Hunter, Gen. Slocum, H. Walley. Nichols and Jennings, residents and property owners on Clinton avenue, protested against the proposed route through Waverly avenue.

Messrs. Corrigan, McGeehan, Linton, J. P. Darling, Pickering, Jere Johnson, Supervisor Tarbell, and Mr. Rapelye spoke in favor of a continuation of the Kings County road to the present City line, but proposed changes in the route. There was no objection to this road.

The hearing of persons interested in the route through Joralemon Street, thence through Court to Atlantic, through Atlantic to Furman Street to Montague Street Bridge, and also the Third avenue route, was adjourned to Tuesday, March 27th, at 8 o'clock P. M., at same place.

On motion the Commission adjourned to Saturday, March 24th, at 9 A. M. at Room No. 6. Hall of Records.

      GEORGE W. BROWN,
          Secretary.

     COMMISSIONERS OF RAPID TRANSIT,
      City of Brooklyn,
        Room No. 6, Hall of Records,
         Saturday, March 24th, 1888, 9 A. M.

The Board met pursurant to adjournment.

Present—Commissioners Thomas S. Moore, George W. Almy, George W. Brown and Thomas H. McGrath.

The reading of the minutes was dispensed with.

There was general discussion as to routes

On motion adjourned to Monday March 26th, 1888, at 4:30 P. M.

      GEORGE W. BROWN,
         Secretary.

Commissioners of Rapid Transit,
City of Brooklyn,
Room No. 6, Hall of Records,
Monday, March 26, 1888, 4.30 P. M.

The Board met pursuant to adjournment.

Present—Commissioners Thomas S. Moore, George W. Almy, George W. Brown and Thomas H. McGrath.

The minutes of the meetings of March 20th, 21st, 23d and 24th insts. were read and approved.

There was general discussion as to routes.

Adjourned to Tuesday, March 27th, 1888, at 8 o'clock P. M.

GEORGE W. BROWN,
Secretary.

Commissioners of Rapid Transit,
City of Brooklyn,
Surrogate's Court Room, Hall of Records,
Tuesday, March 27, 1888, 8 P. M.

The Board met pursuant to adjournment.

Present—Commissioners Thomas S. Moore, George W. Almy, George W. Brown, Thomas H. McGrath and Eugene Doherty.

The reading of the minutes was dispensed with.

Objections to the Court street portion of the proposed route from Fulton street to South Ferry were presented by Messrs. Theodore B. Willets, Andrew Doherty, Charles A. Silva, James B. Healey, Henry Heims, Frederick Stock, J. S.

VanCleaf, James J. Garvey, Robert L. Waterbury, Evan J. Rustin, John F. Nelson, J. S. Parker, John G. Opitz, George Patterson, George Williamson, II. J. Brandt, Frederick S. Otis and Joseph Huhm, representing property owners and residents on Court street.

Mr. Tunis G. Bergen presented a certified copy of a remonstrance against the proposed route on Third avenue.

Mr. Walter Thorne spoke in favor of the Third avenue route.

On motion, the Board adjourned to March 28th, 4.30 P. M.

GEORGE W. BROWN,
Secretary.

COMMISSIONERS OF RAPID TRANSIT,
City of Brooklyn,
Room No. 6, Hall of Records.
Wednesday, March 28, 1888, 4.30 P. M.

The Board met pursuant to notice.

Present—Commissioners George W. Almy, George W. Brown and Eugene Doherty.

In the absence of the chairman, Commissioner Almy called the meeting to order, and was elected temporary chairman.

The minutes of the meetings of March 26th and 27th were read and approved.

There was general discussson as to routes.

Adjourned to Thursday, March 29th, at 5 P. M.

Commissioner Moore came in after adjournment.

GEORGE W. BROWN,
Secretary.

Commissioners of Rapid Transit,
City of Brooklyn,
Room No. 6, Hall of Records,
March 29th, 1888, 5 p. m.

The Board met pursuant to adjournment.

Present—Commissioners Thomas S. Moore, George W. Almy and Eugene Doherty.

The minutes of March 28th were read and approved.

Adjourned to meet March 30th, at 9 a. m. at the office of the Secretary, 416 Bedford Avenue for the purpose of inspecting the proposed routes.

GEORGE W. BROWN,
Secretary.

Commissioners of Rapid Transit,
City of Brooklyn,
Office of Commissioner Brown,
416 Bedford Avenue,
Friday, March 30, 1888, 9 a. m.

The Board met pursuant to adjournment.

Present—Commissioners Thomas S. Moore, George W. Almy, George W. Brown, Thomas H. McGrath and Eugene Doherty, also the Engineer.

The reading of the minutes was dispensed with.

After some discussion the Commissioners and Engineer drove over the various streets and avenues covering what is known as Route 1, commencing at Newtown Creek and ending at the Brighton Beach Depot, corner of Franklin Avenue and Bergen Street.

Adjourned to March 31, at 9 a. m.

GEORGE W. BROWN,
Secretary.

COMMISSIONERS OF RAPID TRANSIT,
City of Brooklyn,
Room No. 6, Hall of Records,
Saturday, March 31, 1888, 9 A. M.

The Board met pursurant to adjournment.

Present—Commissioners Thomas S. Moore, George W. Almy, George W. Brown, Thomas H. McGrath and Eugene Doherty, and the Engineer Mr. Probasco.

The reading of the minutes was dispensed with.

There was general discussion as to routes

Adjourned to Monday, April 2, at 5 P. M.

GEORGE W. BROWN,
Secretary.

COMMISSIONERS OF RAPID TRANSIT,
City of Brooklyn,
Room No. 6, Hall of Records,
Monday, April 2, 1888, 5 P. M.

No quorum being present the Commission adjourned to Tuesday, April 3, 1888, at 9 A. M.

GEORGE W. BROWN,
Secretary.

COMMISSIONERS OF RAPID TRANSIT,
City of Brooklyn,
Room No. 6, Hall of Records,
Tuesday, April 3, 1888, 9 A. M.

The Board met pursuant to adjournment.

Present—Commissioners Thomas S. Moore, George W. Almy, George W. Brown and Eugene Doherty, and the Engineer.

The reading of the minutes was dispensed with.

There was general discussion as to routes.

Adjourned to Wednesday, April 4th, at 5 P. M.

GEORGE W. BROWN,
Secretary.

COMMISSIONERS OF RAPID TRANSIT,
City of Brooklyn,
Room No. 6, Hall of Records,
Wednesday, April 4th, 1888, 5 P. M.

The Board met pursuant to adjournment.

Present—Commissioners Thomas S. Moore, George W. Almy, George W. Brown and Eugene Doherty.

The reading of the minutes was dispensed with.

There was general discussion as to routes.

Adjourned to Thursday, April 5th, at 5 P. M.,

GEORGE W. BROWN,
Secretary.

Commissioners of Rapid Transit,
City of Brooklyn,
Room No. 6, Hall of Records,
Thursday, April 5, 1888, 5 p. m.

There being no quorum present the meeting adjourned to Friday, April 6th, at 3 p. m. at the Howard House, East New York, for the purpose of inspecting the proposed routes.

GEORGE W. BROWN,
Secretary.

Commissioners of Rapid Transit,
City of Brooklyn,
Howard House, East New York,
Friday, April 6, 1888, 3 p. m.

The Board met pursuant to adjournment.

Present—Commissioners Thomas S. Moore, George W. Almy, George W. Brown, Thomas H. McGrath, Eugene Doherty and the Engineer.

The reading of the minutes was dispensed with.

After discussion, the Commissioners went over Fulton, Liberty and Baltic avenues, the Eastern Parkway, Williams place, Vesta avenue and many of the cross streets.

Adjourned to April 7th, 1888, at 9 a. m.

GEORGE W. BROWN,
Secretary.

COMMISSIONERS OF RAPID TRANSIT,
City of Brooklyn,
Room No. 6, Hall of Records,
Saturday, April 7, 1888, 9 A. M.

The Board met pursuant to adjournment.

Present—Commissioners Thomas S. Moore, George W. Almy, George W. Brown, Thomas H. McGrath, Eugene Doherty, and the Engineer.

The reading of the minutes was dispensed with.

The Secretary presented a protest from property owners on Liberty avenue, against the use of that avenue for Elevated Railroads, on account of late expenditures in paving, and urged a parallel avenue, which was received and placed on file.

There was general discussion as to routes.

Adjourned to Monday, April 9, 1888, at 4.30 P. M.

GEORGE W. BROWN,
Secretary.

COMMISSIONERS OF RAPID TRANSIT,
City of Brooklyn,
Room No. 6, Hall of Records,
Monday, April 9, 1888, 4.30 P. M.

The Board met pursuant to adjournment.

Present—Commissioners George W. Almy, George W. Brown, Thomas H. McGrath and Eugene Doherty.

Commissioner Almy was elected Chairman, *pro tem.*

The minutes of the meetings of March 29th, 30th and 31st, and the 2d, 3d, 4th, 5th, 6th and 7th insts., were read and approved.

There was general discussion as to proposed routes.

Adjourned to April 10, at 5 P. M.

GEORGE W. BROWN,
Secretary.

COMMISSIONERS OF RAPID TRANSIT,
City of Brooklyn,
Room No. 6, Hall of Records,
Tuesday, April 10, 1888, 5 P. M.

The Board met pursuant to adjournment.

Present—Commissioners George W. Almy, George W. Brown, Thomas H. McGrath, Eugene Doherty and the Engineer.

Commissioner Almy was elected Chairman *pro tem.*

The reading of the minutes was dispensed with.

There was a lengthy discussion as to the proposed routes.

Adjourned to Wednesday, April 11, at 4.30 P. M.

GEORGE W. BROWN,
Secretary.

COMMISSIONERS OF RAPID TRANSIT,
City of Brooklyn,
Room No. 6, Hall of Records,
Wednesday, April 11, 1888, 4.30 P. M.

The Board met pursuant to adjournment.

Present—Commissioners George W. Almy, George W. Brown, Thomas H. McGrath, and Eugene Doherty, and the Engineer.

Commissioner Almy was elected temporary Chairman.

The minutes of the meetings of April 9th and 10th were read and approved.

A protest from residents on William's avenue, protesting against the use of that avenue for an Elevated Railroad, was received and placed on file.

A long discussion as to routes followed.

Adjourned to Thursday, April 12th, 1888, at 1.30 P. M.

GEORGE W. BROWN,
Secretary.

COMMISSIONERS OF RAPID TRANSIT,
City of Brooklyn,
Room No. 6, Hall of Records,
Thursday, April 12, 1888, 1.30 P. M.

The Board met pursuant to adjournment.

Present—Thomas S. Moore, George W. Almy, George W. Brown, Thomas H. McGrath, Eugene Doherty and the Engineer,

The reading of the minutes was dispensed with.

Commissioner Brown offered the following routes for the consideration of the Commission:

ROUTE I.

Beginning on and over Manhattan avenue, at or near its intersection with Newtown Creek; running thence over, through and along Manhattan avenue to Commercial street; thence over, through and along Commercial street to Franklin street; thence over, through and along Franklin street to Kent avenue; thence over, through and along Kent avenue to Myrtle avenue.

ROUTE II.

Beginning on and over Fulton street at its intersection with the former boundary line, between the City of Brooklyn and the Town of New Lots; thence over, through and along Fulton street to Jamaica avenue; thence over, through and along Jamaica avenue to any point on said avenue east of Vesta avenue (formerly Van Sindaren avenue) and west of William's place; thence over, through and across private property to and across Herkimer street; thence over, through and along Herkimer street to William's place; thence over, through and along William's place to, over and across East New York avenue and Atlantic avenue to Snedeker avenue; thence over, through and along Snedeker avenue to the Eastern Parkway; thence over, through and along the Eastern Parkway to Market street; thence over, through and along Market street to Liberty avenue; thence over, through and along Liberty avenue to the boundary line, between the City of Brooklyn and the Town of Jamaica.

Provided that the Company authorized to build, or which may acquire the right to build a railway or railways upon said above described route, may build the same wholly upon said described route, or may vary the same as follows:

Beginning on and over Fulton street at its intersection with the former boundary line between the City of Brooklyn and the Town of New Lots; running thence over, through and along Fulton street to Jamaica avenue; thence over, through and along Jamaica avenue to Williams place; thence over, through and along Williams place to, over and across East New York avenue and Atlantic avenue to Snedeker avenue; thence over, through and along Snedeker avenue to the Eastern Parkway; thence over, through and along the Eastern Parkway to Market street; thence over, through and along Market street to Liberty avenue; thence over, through and along Liberty avenue to the boundary line between the City of Brooklyn and the Town of Jamaica

Or said Company may vary the route as follows:

Beginning on and over Fulton street at its intersection with the former boundary line between the City of Brooklyn and the Town of New Lots; running thence over, through and along Fulton street to Jamaica avenue; thence over, through and along Jamaica avenue to, and across East New York avenue to Alabama avenue; thence over, through and along Alabama avenue to the Eastern Parkway; thence over, through and along the Eastern Parkway to Market street; thence over, through and along Market street to Liberty avenue; thence over, through and along Liberty avenue to the boundary line between the City of Brooklyn and the Town of Jamaica.

Adjourned to Friday, April 13, 1888, at 9 A. M.

GEORGE W. BROWN,
Secretary.

COMMISSIONERS OF RAPID TRANSIT,
City of Brooklyn,
Room No. 6, Hall of Records,
Friday, April 13, 1888, 9 A. M.

The Board met pursuant to adjournment.

Present—Thomas S. Moore, George W. Almy, George W. Brown, Thomas H. McGrath and Eugene Doherty.

The minutes of the meetings of April 11th and 12th were read and approved.

A protest from property owners on Court street, protesting against an elevated railway on that street, was received and placed on file.

There was general discussion as to the routes proposed on the 12th inst.

Adjourned to 4.30 P. M., to-day.

GEORGE W. BROWN,
Secretary.

COMMISSIONERS OF RAPID TRANSIT,
City of Brooklyn,
Room No. 6, Hall of Records,
Friday, April 13, 1888, 4.30 P. M.

The Board met pursuant to adjournment.

Present—Commissioners Thomas S. Moore, George W. Almy, George W. Brown and Thomas H. McGrath.

The reading of the minutes was dispensed with.

Commissioner Brown proposed the following as a substitute for the second alternative route. "Or said Company may vary said route as follows; beginning at the intersection of Broadway and Alabama avenue; running thence over, through and along Alabama to the Eastern Parkway; thence over, through and along the Eastern Parkway to Market street; thence over, through and along Market street to Liberty avenue; thence over, through and along Liberty avenue to the boundary line between the City of Brooklyn and the town of Jamacia."

Adjourned to Saturday, April 14, 1888, at 9 A. M.

GEORGE W. BROWN,
Secretary.

COMMISSIONERS OF RAPID TRANSIT,
City of Brooklyn,
Room No. 6, Hall of Records,
Saturday, April 14, 1888, 9 A. M

The Board met pursuant to adjournment.

Present—Commissioners Thomas S. Moore, George W. Almy, George W. Brown, Thomas H. McGrath and Eugene Doherty.

The minutes of the two meetings on the 13th were read and approved.

On motion of Commissioner Almy,

Resolved, That in pursuance of the powers conferred upon us by Chapter 606 of the Laws of 1875, and the acts amendatory thereof, we, the Commissioners appointed by the Mayor of the City of Brooklyn, on the 4th day of February, 1888, do hereby fix and determine the route or routes of a steam railway or railways in the City of Brooklyn, as follows :

Route I.

Beginning on and over Manhattan avenue at or near its intersection with Newtown Creek; running thence over, through and along Manhattan avenue to Commercial street; thence over, through and along Commercial street to Franklin street; thence over, through and along Franklin street to Kent avenue; thence over, through and and along Kent avenue to Myrtle avenue.

Commissioners Moore, Almy, Brown and McGrath, voted in favor of this resolution; Commissioner Doherty voted against it.

The resolution was declared carried.

On motion of Commissioner Almy:

Resolved, That in pursuance of the powers conferred upon us by Chapter 606 of the Laws of 1875, and the acts amendatory thereof, we, the Commissioners, appointed by the Mayor of the City of Brooklyn, on the 4th day of February, 1888, do hereby fix and determine the route or routes of a steam railway or railways in the City of Brooklyn, as follows:

Route II.

Beginning on and over Fulton street, at its intersection with the former boundary line, between the City of Brooklyn and the town of New Lots; thence over, through and along Fulton street to Jamaica avenue; thence over, through and along Jamaica avenue, to any point on said avenue, east of Vesta avenue (formerly Van Sindaren avenue), and west of Williams place; thence over, through and across private property to and across Herkimer street; thence over, through and along Herkimer street to Williams place; thence over, through and along Williams place to and across East New York avenue and Atlantic avenue to Snedeker avenue; thence over, through and along Snedeker avenue to the Eastern Parkway; thence over, through and along the Eastern Parkway to Market street; thence over, through and along Market street to Liberty avenue; thence over, through and along Liberty avenue to the boundary line between the City of Brooklyn and the Town of Jamaica.

Provided that the Company authorized to build or which may acquire the right to build a railway or railways upon said above described route may build the same wholly upon said described route or may vary the same as follows:

Beginning on and over Fulton street, at its intersection with the former boundary line between the City of Brooklyn and the Town of New Lots; running thence over, through and along Fulton street to Jamaica avenue; thence over, through and along Jamaica avenue to Williams place; thence over, through and along Williams place to, over and across East New York avenue and Atlantic avenue to Snedeker Avenue; thence over, through and along Snedeker avenue to the Eastern Parkway; thence over, through and along the Eastern Parkway to Market street; thence over, through and along Market street to Liberty avenue; thence over, through and along Liberty avenue to the boundary line between the City of Brooklyn and the Town of Jamaica.

Or said Company may vary said route as follows:

Beginning on and over Fulton street, at its intersection with the former boundary line between the City of Brooklyn and the Town of New Lots; running thence over, through and along Fulton street to Jamaica avenue; thence over, through and along Jamaica avenue, to and across East New York avenue to Alabama avenue; thence over, through and along Alabama avenue to the Eastern Parkway; thence over, through and along the Eastern Parkway to Market street; thence over, through and along Market street to Liberty avenue; thence over, through and along Liberty avenue to the boundary line between the City of Brooklyn and the Town of Jamaica.

Adopted unanimously.

On motion of Commissioner Almy, the following resolution was adopted :

Resolved, That the location of the routes hereinabove designated and of each thereof, shall and does include the right to construct, use and operate in connection therewith the usual necessary depots, tracks, stairways, sidings, turnouts, curves, switches, platforms and other appurtenances incidental to the construction, operation and maintenance of elevated railroads, and to use and occupy the portions of the various streets under or adjacent to said road for that purpose.

*Resolved, That said corporation shall not be required to build or operate a railway upon any portion of any route fixed by these Commissioners as aforesaid, upon which any other corporation duly authorized to do so, shall have built or operated a railway.

Resolved, That whenever either of the routes hereinbefore fixed and determined crosses any street, avenue, place or lands, such route includes and is intended to include such crossing and so much of said street, avenue, place or land as is there crossed, as will allow and enable the construction of continuous connected lines of railway along the routes so crossing.

Resolved, That whenever either of the routes hereinbefore fixed and determined is stated to commence, pass or end at the intersection of any street or avenue upon which a route or routes have been by this Commission fixed and determined, or upon which any elevated railroad has been constructed, or where any such route or routes commence pass or terminate on the opposite side of any such street or avenue, such route or routes shall be deemed to commence, p iss or end as the case may be, at the railway which shall be constructed on such street or avenue at which such route begins, passes or ends, so as to allow and permit of a connection between the railways projected or constructed on

* NOTE—Rescinded by resolution adopted May 25th. See page —

each of said intersecting streets or avenues, including such curves as may be necessary for that purpose.

On motion, the Board adjourned to Monday, April 16, 1888, at 9 A. M.

GEORGE W. BROWN,
Secretary.

COMMISSIONERS OF RAPID TRANSIT,
City of Brooklyn,
Room No. 6. Hall of Records,
Monday, April 16, 1888, 9 A. M.

The Board met pursuant to adjournment.

Present—Commissioners Thomas S. Moore, George W. Almy, George W. Brown and Eugene Doherty.

The minutes of the meeting of the 14th inst. were read and approved.

On motion of Commissioner Brown the following resolution was adopted:

Resolved, That the Secretary be and is hereby directed to forward to the Mayor of the City of Brooklyn a copy of the resolutions establishing routes adopted by this Board on the 14th inst.

On motion of Commissioner Almy the following resolution was adopted:

Resolved, That the Secretary be instructed to publish the following notice in the Brooklyn *Daily Eagle*, Brooklyn *Standard-Union*, Brooklyn *Times*, Brooklyn *Frie Presse*, Brooklyn *Citizen*, and the Brooklyn edition of the New York *World*, three times a week from the 17th day of April, 1888, until the 29th day of April, 1888, inclusive, viz:

NOTICE.

OFFICE OF COMMISSIONERS OF RAPID TRANSIT,
City of Brooklyn,
Room No. 6, Hall of Records,
April 16, 1888.

The Commissioners appointed by the Mayor of the City of Brooklyn on the 4th day of February 1888, under and in compliance with the provisions of Chapter 606 of the Laws of 1875, and the acts amendatory thereof, hereby give notice that the submission of plans for the construction and operation of Rapid Transit Railways authorized by said act is hereby invited. Such plans must be shown by drawings or models and accompanied by descriptions in writing, if descriptions are to be made. The Commissioners request the attendance before the Board of the person or persons submitting plans which require explanation and description more in detail than the description accompanying the plans when submitted. It is requested that such plans shall be submitted as early as convenient and on or before the 30th day of April, 1888, at 9 A. M., at their office, Room No. 6, Hall of Records.

The said Commissioners hereby further give notice that the Commissioners will meet at nine o'clock in the forenoon on the 7th day of May, 1888, at their office, Room No. 6, Hall of Records, Fulton Street, and decide upon the plan or plans for the construction of such railway or railways, with the necessary supports, turnouts, switches, sidings, connections, landing places, stations, buildings, platforms, stairways, elevators, telegraph and signal devices, and other requisite appliances upon the route or routes, heretofore determined upon by them, which routes are as follows:—

ROUTE I.

Beginning on and over Manhattan avenue at or near its intersection with Newtown Creek; running thence, over, through and along Manhattan avenue to Commercial street; thence over, through and along Commercial street to Franklin street; thence over, through and along Franklin street; to Kent avenue; thence over, through and along Kent avenue to Myrtle avenue.

ROUTE II.

Beginning on and over Fulton street at its intersection with the former boundary line between the City of Brooklyn and the town of New Lots; thence ove, through and along Jamaica avenue to any point on said avenue east of Vesta avenue (formerly Van Sindaren avenue) and west of Williams place; thence over, through and across private property to and across Herkimer street; thence over, through and along Herkimer street to Williams place; thence over, through and along Williams place to, over and across East New York avenue and Atlantic avenue to Snedeker avenue; thence over, through and along Snedeker avenue to the Eastern Parkway; thence over, through and along the Eastern Parkway to Market street; thence over, through and along Market street to Liberty avenue; thence over, through and along Liberty avenue to the boundary line between the City of Brooklyn and the town of Jamaica.

Provided that the Company authorized to build or which may acquire the right to build a railway or railways upon said above described route may build the same wholly upon said described route, or may vary the same as follows:

Beginning on and over Fulton street at its intersection with the former boundary line between the City of Brooklyn and the town of New Lots; running thence over, through and along Fulton street to Jamaica avenue; thence over, through and along Jamaica avenue to Williams place; thence over, through and along Williams place to, over and across East New York avenue and Atlantic avenue to Snedeker avenue; thence over, through and along Snedeker avenue to the Eastern Parkway; thence over, through and along the Eastern Parkway to Market street; thence over, through and along Market street to Liberty avenue; thence over, through and along Liberty avenue to the boundary line between the City of Brooklyn and the town of Jamaica.

Or said Company may vary said route as follows: Beginning on and over Fulton street at its intersection with the former boundary line between the City of Brooklyn and the town of New Lots; running thence over, through and along Fulton street to Jamaica avenue; thence over, through and along Jamaica avenue to and across East New York avenue to Alabama avenue; thence over, through and along Alabama avenue to the Eastern Parkway; thence over, through and along the Eastern Parkway to Market street; thence over, through and along Market street to Liberty avenue; thence over, through and along Liberty avenue to the boundary line between the City of Brooklyn and the town of Jamaica.

On motion adjourned to Tuesday, April 17, 1888, at 9 A. M.

GEORGE W. BROWN,
Secretary.

COMMISSIONERS OF RAPID TRANSIT,
City of Brooklyn,
Room No. 6, Hall of Records,
Tuesday, April 17, 1888, 9 A. M.

The Board met pursuant to adjournment.

Present—Commissioners Thomas S. Moore, George W. Almy, George W. Brown and Eugene Doherty.

The minutes of the meeting of the 16th inst. were read and approved.

There was general discussion as to plans and other matters of interest to the Board.

Adjourned to Saturday, April 21, 1888, at 9 A. M.

GEORGE W. BROWN,
Secretary.

Commissioners of Rapid Transit,
City of Brooklyn,
Room No. 6, Hall of Records,
Saturday, April 21, 1888, 9 A. M.

The Board met pursuant to adjournment.

Present—Commissioners Thomas S. Moore, George W. Almy, George W. Brown and Eugene Doherty.

The minutes of the meeting of the 17th inst. were read and approved.

The Secretary reported publishing the resolution as directed in the meeting of the Board held on the 16th inst., in the *Brooklyn Daily Eagle*, *Brooklyn Standard Union*, *Brooklyn Times*, *Brooklyn Freie Presse*, *Brooklyn Citizen*, and Brooklyn edition of the *New York World*.

There was general discussion upon matters of interest to the Board.

Adjourned to Tuesday, April 24, 1888, at 9 A. M.

GEORGE W. BROWN,
Secretary.

Commissioners of Rapid Transit,
City of Brooklyn,
Room No. 6, Hall of Records,
Tuesday, April 24, 1888, 9 A. M.

The Board met pursuant to adjournment.

Present—Commissioners Thomas S. Moore, George W. Almy, George W. Brown, Thomas H. McGrath and Eugene Doherty.

The minutes of the meeting of the 21st inst. were read and approved.

There was general discussion upon matters connected with the Commission.

Adjourned to Thursday, April 26, 1888, at 5 P. M.

GEORGE W. BROWN,
Secretary.

COMMISSIONERS OF RAPID TRANSIT,
City of Brooklyn,
Room 6, Hall of Records.
Thursday, April 26, 1888, 5 P. M.

The Board met pursuant to adjournment.

Present—Commissioners George W. Almy, George W. Brown, Thomas H. McGrath, Eugene Doherty and the Engineer.

Reading of the minutes was dispensed with.

Commissioner Almy was elected Chairman.

There was general discussion upon matters of interest to the Board.

Adjourned to Friday, April 27, at 5 P. M.

GEORGE W. BROWN,
Secretary.

COMMISSIONERS OF RAPID TRANSIT,
City of Brooklyn,
Room No. 6, Hall of Records,
Friday, April 27, 1888, 5 P. M.

The Board met pursuant to adjournment.

Present—Commissioner Thomas S. Moore, George W. Almy, George W. Brown, Thomas H. McGrath and the Engineer.

Minutes of the meetings of the 24th and 26th inst. were read and approved.

There was lengthy discussion as to plans.

Adjourned to Monday, April 30, 1888, at 9 A. M.

GEORGE W. BROWN,
Secretary.

COMMISSIONERS OF RAPID TRANSIT,
City of Brooklyn,
Room No. 6, Hall of Records,
Monday, April 30, 1888, 9 A. M.

The Board met pursuant to adjournment.

Present—Commissioners Thomas S. Moore, George W. Almy, George W. Brown, Thomas H. McGrath and the Engineer.

Minutes of the meeting of the 27th inst. were read and approved.

The chair announced that the Board was ready for the submission of plans for construction.

Gen. Jourdan submitted a plan for the proposed roads with drawings and specifications. The same were received and examined and referred to the engineer, Mr. Probasco, for further consideration.

Adjourned to Tuesday, May 1, 1888, at 4.30 P. M.

GEORGE W. BROWN,
Secretary.

COMMISSIONERS OF RAPID TRANSIT,
City of Brooklyn,
Room No. 6, Hall of Records,
Tuesday, May 1, 1888, 4.30 P. M.

The Board met pursuant to adjournment.

Present—Commissioners Thomas S. Moore, George W. Almy, George W. Brown and Eugene Doherty.

Minutes of the meeting of the 30th ult. were read and approved.

There was general discussion upon matters of interest to the Board.

Adjourned to Wednesday, May 2, 1888, at 4.30 P. M.

GEORGE W. BROWN,
Secretary.

Commissioners of Rapid Transit,
City of Brooklyn,
Room No. 6, Hall of Records,
Wednesday, May 2, 1888, 4.30 p. m.

The Board met pursuant to adjournment.

Present—Commissioners George W. Almy, George W. Brown, Eugene Doherty and the Engineer.

On motion of Commissioner Doherty Commissioner Almy was elected Chairman *pro tem.*

Reading of the minutes was dispensed with.

There was discussion regarding the plans presented at the last meeting.

Adjourned to Friday, May 4th, 1888, at 4.30 p. m.

GEORGE W. BROWN,
Secretary.

Commissioners of Rapid Transit,
City of Brooklyn,
Room No. 6, Hall of Records,
Friday, May 4th, 1888, 4.30 p. m.

The Board met pursuant to adjournment.

Present—Commissioners George W. Almy, George W. Brown, Eugene Doherty and the Engineer.

Commissioner Almy was elected temporary Chairman.

The minutes of the 1st and 2d insts. were read and approved.

The Engineer presented requirements and conditions to be imposed by the Board of Rapid Transit Commissioners upon the Company, which shall hereafter be organized to construct the railways adopted by the Board.

Adjourned to Monday, May 7th, 1888, at 9 a. m.

GEORGE W. BROWN,
Secretary.

Commissioners of Rapid Transit,
City of Brooklyn,
Room No. 6, Hall of Records,
Monday, May 7, 1888, 9 a. m.

The Board met pursuant to adjournment.

Present—Commissioners Thomas S. Moore, George W. Almy, George W. Brown, Eugene Doherty and the Engineer.

The minutes of the meeting of May 4th, read and approved.

The Engineer produced maps and plans, and after lengthy discussion, on motion of Commissioner Doherty the following resolution was unanimously adopted.

Resolved, That the Commissioners appointed by the Mayor of the City of Brooklyn, on the 4th day of February, 1888, under and in compliance with the provisions of Chapter 606, of the Laws of 1875, and the act or acts amendatory thereof, having by such public notice as they deem most proper and effective, invited the submission of plans for the construction and operation of a railway or railways, for the purpose provided for by said acts, and having examined and considered the plans and devices submitted to them, do hereby select and decide upon plans for the construction of such railway or railways with the necessary supports, turnouts, switches, sidings, stations, buildings, platforms, telegraph and signal devices, and other requisite appliances upon the route or routes, in the locations determined upon by them, by resolutions adopted on the 14th day of April, 1888, as follows:

First. The plans as shown upon the maps herewith filed and maked respectively A, B, C, D, E and F, and signed by the Secretary and Engineer of the Commission.

Second. The general plan of construction, as follows:

GENERAL PLAN AND SPECIFICATIONS FOR AN ELEVATED RAILWAY.

1. The general plan or plans of the structure shall be of an Elevated Railway, suported upon a row or rows of columns; the track or tracks shall be carried by longitudinal girders, resting either upon the tops of the columns or upon transverse girders suported by the columns.

2. Where the width of the street between the curbstones does not exceed forty feet, the plan of construction shall be as follows, to wit, with a row of columns on the line of each curb, and a superstructure carrying the tracks upon transverse girders spanning the street.

3. Where the width of the street or avenue between the curbstones is more than forty feet, the plan of construction shall be as follows, as the company constructing the railway shall elect, *i. e.*, either *First*, with a row of columns upon the line of each curb and a superstructure carring the tracts upon transverse girders spanning the street; or, *Second*, with two rows of columns in the roadway of the street and a superstructure carrying the tracks either upon transverse girders or over each row of columns; but no columns authorized in this plan of construction shall be erected on any avenue or street except in the Twenty-sixth Ward and on the street or avenue known as Eastern Parkway.

4. Whenever a column or a row of columns is above authorized to be upon a line of curb, such columns or row of columns shall be erected only within the line of curbstones, and shall be there so situated and placed as not to obstruct vehicles or the ordinary trafic or travel of the roadway or street.

5. There shall not be more than two rows of columns or more than two tracks in any one street or avenue or public place, except as hereinafter authorized.

6. No colums shall be erected between any two tracks or street railroad, now upon the surface of the roadway of the street, except, as herein otherwise authorized.

7. Except where the width of a cross street, between the curbs thereof, is forty feet or more, every cross street shall be spanned by a single span, when and where the plan of construction used is one having a row of columns upon a curb line.

8. The transverse diameter of a column authorized to be in the roadway of any street shall not exceed eighteen inches at the base and thence for at least ten feet above the surface of the roadway; and the transverse diameter of a column authorized to be on the line of a curb, shall not exceed twenty-six inches at the base and thence for at least ten feet above the surface of the roadway.

9. When and where the plan of construction used is one having two columns in the roadway of the street, no column shall be erected between the curb lines of a cross street, elsewhere than upon the centre line of such cross street, but may be there erected when the distance between curbs exceeds forty feet.

10. A single or double track may be placed between longitudinal girders and carried by iron floor beams, the latter supported by the longitudinal girders.

11. Where columns are authorized to be in the roadway on each side of a street railroad track upon the surface of the roadway the transverse distance between the column shall be at least twenty-one feet in the clear.

12. Where two rows of columns are authorized, and either row is placed in the roadway of the street, the columns shall be erected in pairs and both columns of each pair shall stand in line at right angles to the axis of the street, except on curves.

13. The transverse diameter of columns above indicated does not include fenders; and adequate fenders shall be fitted round the base of each column placed in the roadway to prevent the hubs of the wheels of passing vehicles from striking the columns.

14. The longitudinal distance between columns on the

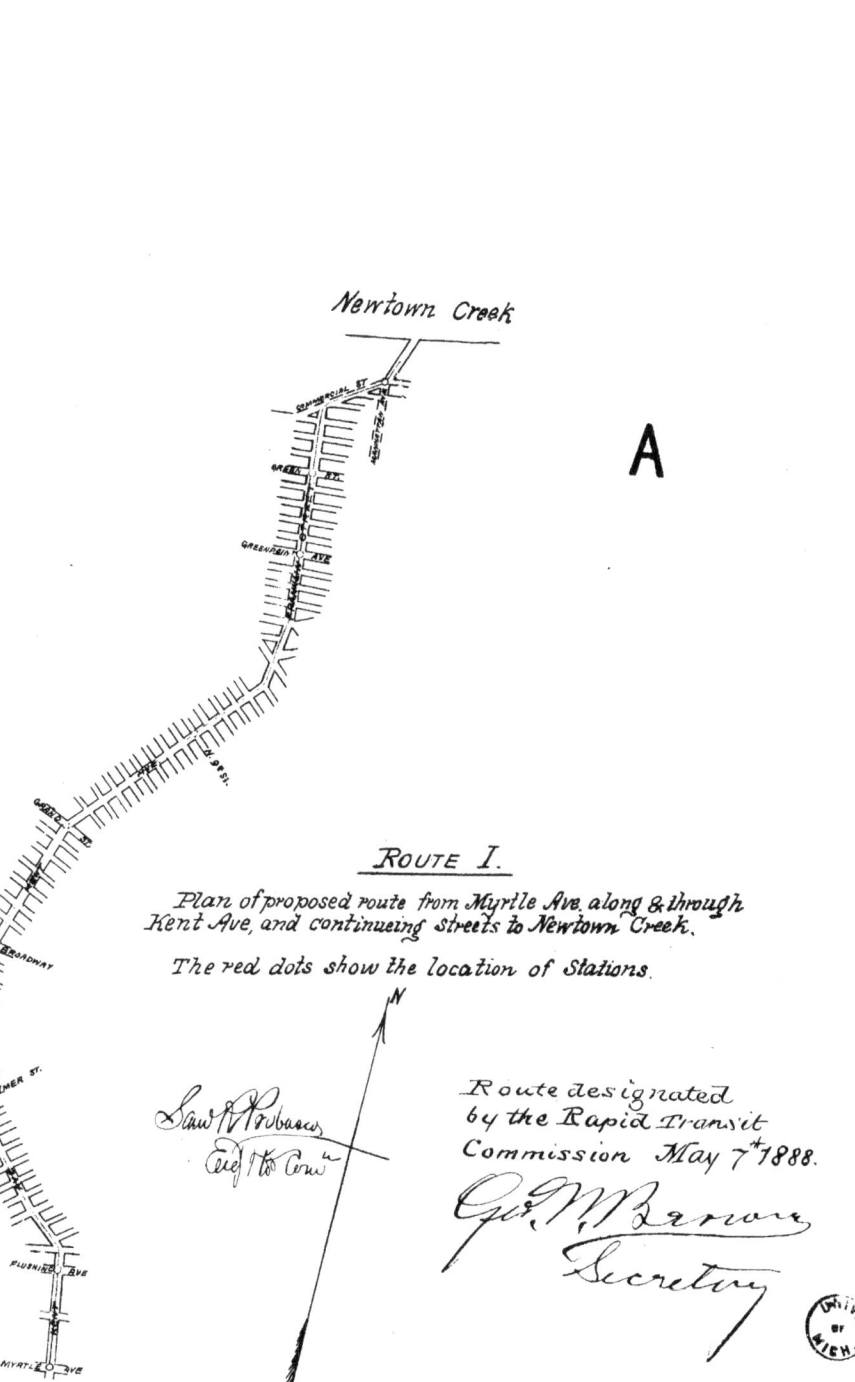

ROUTE II.

Map of Elevated Railway from Sackman Street to County Line on Fulton Avenue and other Streets as shown.

The red dots show the location of Stations

Route designated by the Rapid Transit Commission May 7th 1888.

Front elevation of
Station & Platform.

Accepted by the Rapid
Transit Commission.
May 7th 1888.

C

Scale: 10ft per inch

Route No. 1
Kent Ave., Franklin St. & Comr
and Manhattan Ave.

Sam'l R Probasco (?)
Eng'r ...

Section of main tracks
over 42 ft roadway.

Section of main tracks
and siding over 42 ft roadway.

Above section applicable also to Eastern Parkway
Route No. II

Scale 10 ...

Commercial St,
Ave.

Accepted by the Rapid
Transit Commission
May 7th 1888.

Geo W Brown
Secretary

D

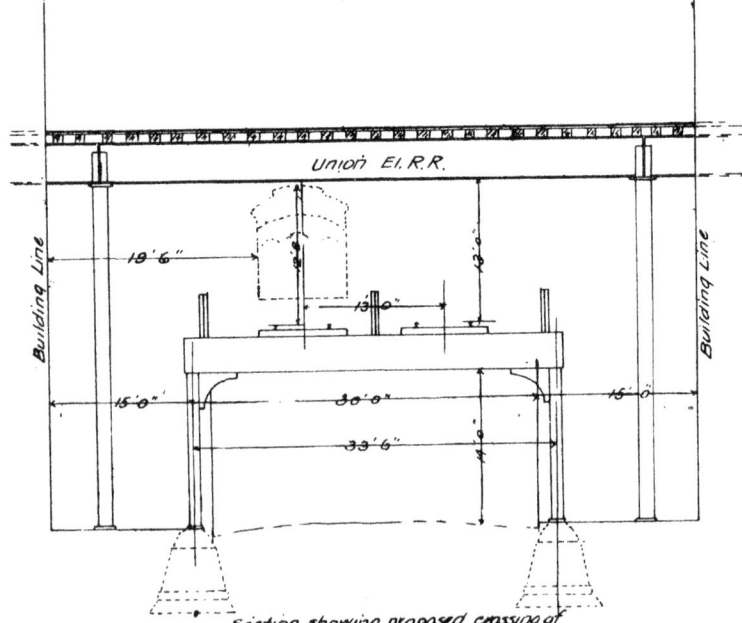

Elevation
50' 0"

Section showing proposed crossing of
BROADWAY
under the Union El. Ry.

Scale 10 ft. per inch.

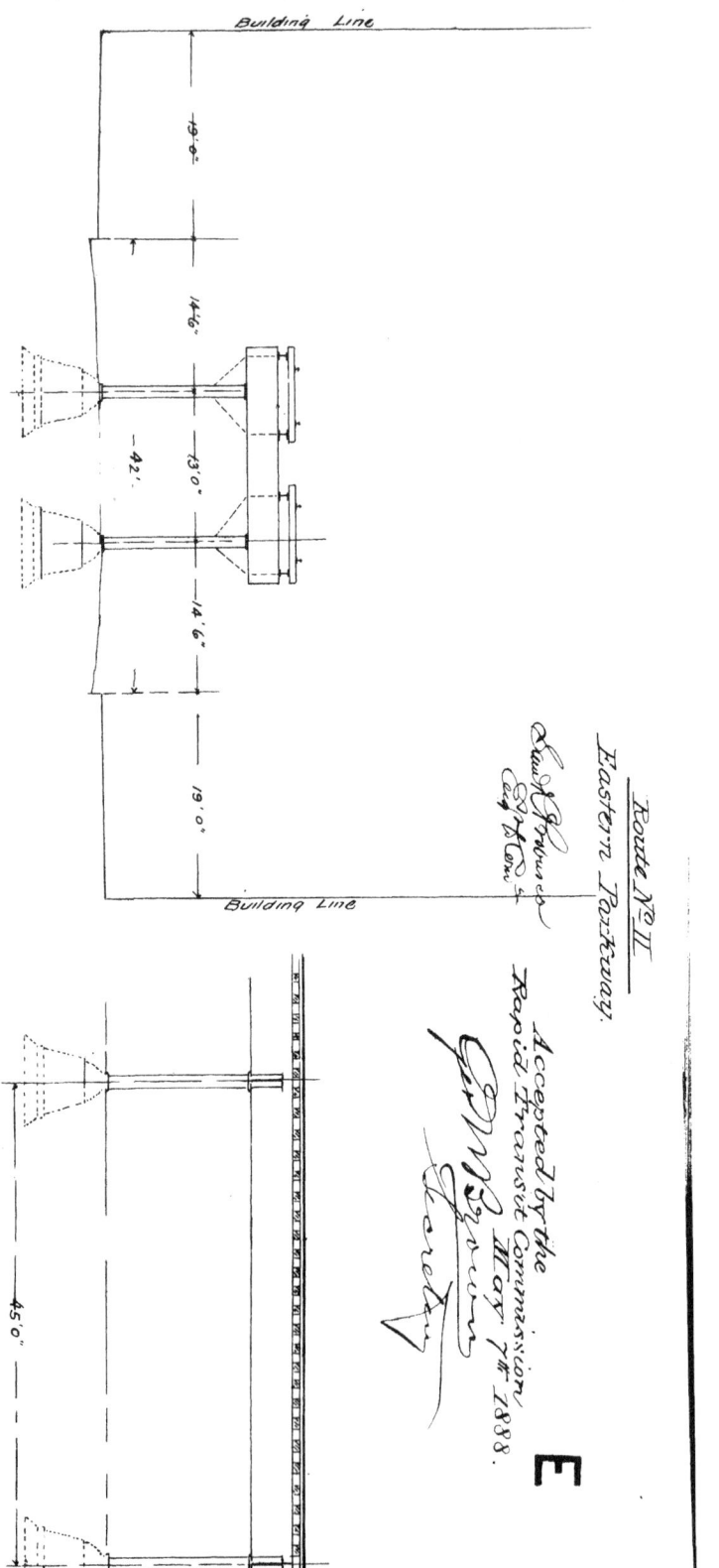

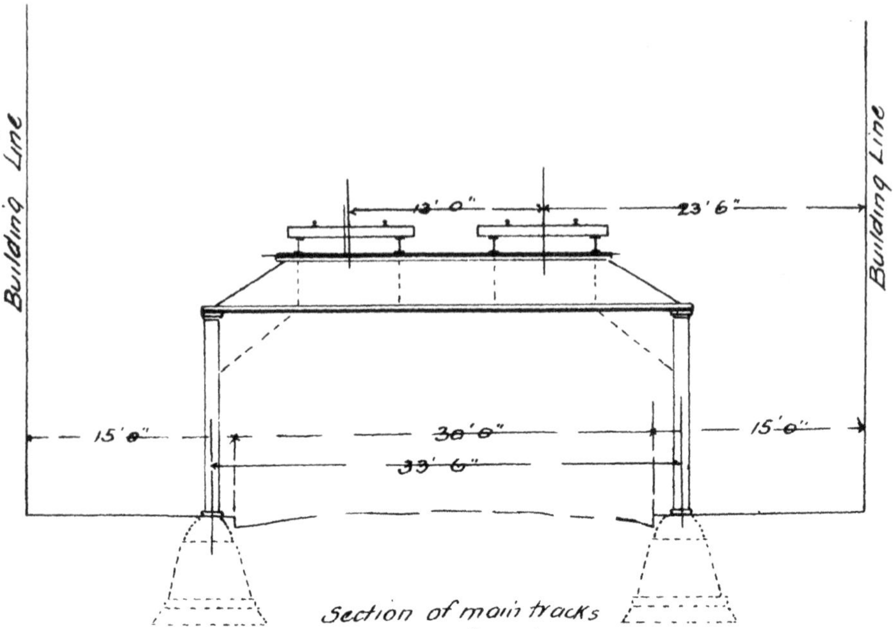

Section of main tracks over 30 ft roadway.

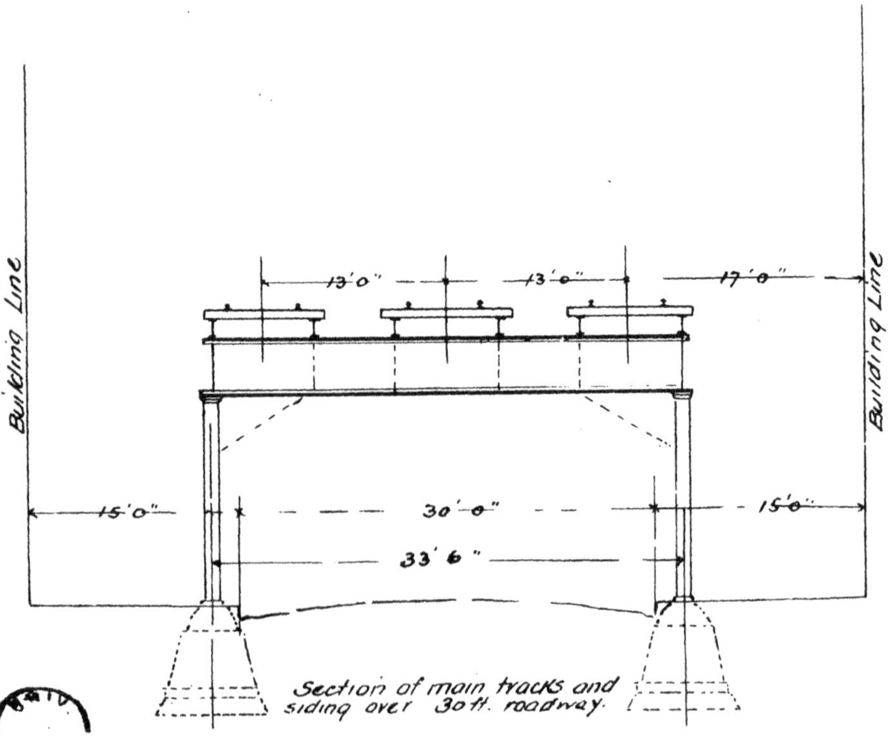

Section of main tracks and siding over 30 ft. roadway.

F

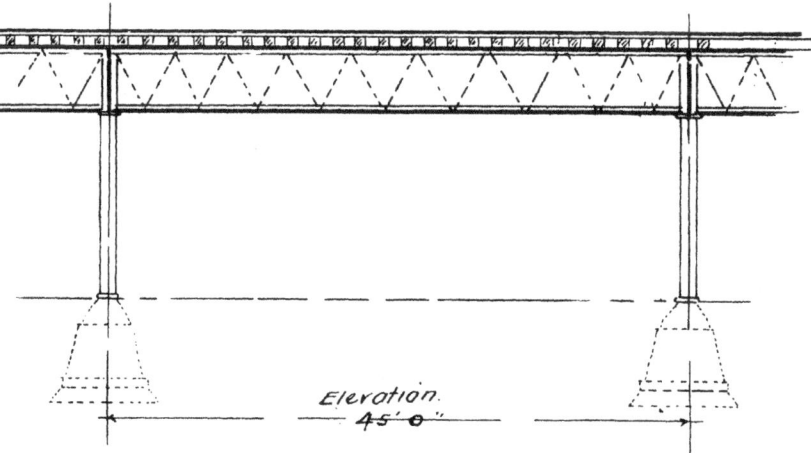

Elevation
45' 0"

Route No II.

Herkimer St., Williams Place, Snediker Ave.
Alabama Ave., Market St., & Liberty Ave.

Accepted by the Rapid Transit
Commission May 7th 1888

Geo W Brown
Secretary

Scale: 10 ft. per inch

curb shall be at least twenty feet. The longitudinal distance between columns in the roadway shall be at least thirty-five feet except as herein otherwise provided.

15. On curves of three hundred feet radius or less, the longitudinal distance between the columns in the roadway may be reduced to not less than twenty-five feet.

16. No part of the girder or superstructure shall be less than fourteen feet above the level of the street.

17. Upon every track there shall be at least four continuous longitudinal stringers of sufficient size, of the best quality of yellow pine timber. The joints of such longitudinal stringers shall be scarfed and bolted, and such stringers shall be securely fastened to each alternate support on which they rest, so as to tie the structure firmly together and give it stiffness in a longitudinal direction, and also act as guard rails. This requirement may be fulfilled either by longitudinal stringers under the rail, or by safety guards of timber, if made to comply with the above conditions.

18. The materials used for that part of the structure above the ground shall be wrought iron or steel—except that the connections between the posts which form a cluster column may be of cast iron—and except the rails which shall be of steel—and except the ties supporting the rails which shall be of the best quality and kind of selected yellow pine timber. The safety guards, if of wood, shall be of the best quality and kind of yellow pine timber. Wood shall not be placed in any position where it may not readily be removed without interrupting the travel on the road.

19. The structure may be built of lattice, or plate girders for the transverse girders, and of lattice girders modified by the use of plates in place of diagonals in the panels near the ends of the girders.

20. The wrought iron shall be of the following general character: Tough, fibrous and uniform in quality, having an elastic limit of 24,000 to 26,000 pounds, and an ultimate tensile strength of 48,000 to 50,000 pounds per square inch

of section ; under tensile strain it shall stretch from 10 to 15 per cent. in 8 inches.

21. All rivets shall be of double refined iron, which shall have an ultimate tensile strength of 60,000 pounds to the square inch. The rivet holes shall be truly and accurately opposite each other ; and the rivets shall enter the holes without drifting or forcing, and shall fill the holes.

22. No part of the structure shall be subjected to a greater strain of tension or compression than 10,000 pounds to the square inch ; and no part shall be subjected to a greater shearing strain than 7,500 pounds to the square inch ; and the structure shall not be proportioned for a less moving load than 2,000 pounds per lineal foot for each track.

23. The maximum deflection of any girder under the passage of a train shall never exceed one fifteen hundredth ($\frac{1}{1500}$) of its length.

24. The angle bars and plates composing the longitudinal parts of a column or girder shall be in single pieces, except in the case of a girder of more than forty feet in length.

25. All parts which make up the section of a column except where cluster columns are used, shall be of equal thickness and uniform quality.

26. The strength of the column shall be proportioned by Gordon's formula for the ratio of the diameter to the length, with five as a factor of safety, or the equivalent thereof.

27. The different parts of the structure and their connections shall be properly proportioned to resist all the strains which the momentum of the train can, by the application of brakes, or in any other manner, impart to the structure.

28. The foundations for the columns shall consist of brick-work of the best quality, except where in water, when the best Rosendale cement concrete, in parts of one

of sand to two of cement to five of broken stone shall be used until a sufficient height is reached above the water when brick-work shall be used.

29. All masonry for foundations shall measure at least three feet square upon the top, at least six feet square at the bottom ; shall not be less than seven feet six inches in depth below the curb. The base shall be a bed of concrete, six inches thick, so as to make a bed for the masonry not less than seven feet square. When the span is more than fifty feet, the dimensions of the foundations shall be larger proportionally.

30. The earth is to be prepared for this masonry by being made firm and solid, and covered with a bed of good hydraulic mortar not less than six inches in depth.

31. Every column or post shall be secured to the masonry by means of a heavy plate of cast iron, so proportioned as to distribute the weight which comes upon it uniformly over the foundation. This plate shall be fastened by sufficiently strong, wrought iron bolts, one and a half inches in diameter—not less than four feet six inches long—the bolts having heads which shall be upset and not welded, and having cast iron socket washers of sufficient size, not less than twelve inches square, built in the masonry. The cast iron plate, its connections with the columns, the wrought iron bolts, and their heads and washers, shall possess sufficient strength to receive and resist equally well with the column all strains which may come upon the latter. The castings shall be of good, tough iron, and before setting shall be thoroughly examined to discover any flaws or imperfections.

32. All the iron work beneath the surface of the street shall be cleaned from rust and scale, and well covered with coal tar varnish before it is set.

33. Good hydraulic cement mortar shall be used in the masonry, of the usual proportions of two parts of sand to one of cement, and fresh burned Rosendale cement of the

first quality shall be used in all cases. The bricks shall be hard burned Haverstraw of the best quality.

34. The foundations, where necessary, shall be increased, in area, so that in no case shall a weight greater than two thousand pounds to the square foot come upon any base.

35. All wrought iron work shall receive, before being riveted together a coat of thick linseed oil and red lead on all surfaces in contact, so that the spaces inclosed shall be completely filled, and shall receive one coat of boiled oil, well brushed on and dried before leaving the shop, and after erection shall receive such covering of paint as to protect all parts of the structure, which shall, where practicable, be accessible for the purpose of painting.

36. Efficient guard rails of iron or wood shall be provided, so that, in case of accident, the cars shall be effectually prevented from leaving the structure.

37. Continuous brakes (either vacuum or pressure), so arrranged as to be under the control of the engineer, shall be applied to all trains, and to every car in each train, as well as efficient hand brakes.

38. All switches shall be split switches of the most approved design, so that if left open or placed wrong, the main track shall not be broken, or offer any impediment which may cause the derailment of a passing train.

39. Rails shall be of steel, not less in weight than fifty-six pounds per lineal yard. They shall be laid and fastened in the most approved manner on cross-ties, 7 inches by 9 inches, laid not over two feet between centres and, when borne by continuous stringers, in addition to the ordinary rail spikes, shall have six three-quarter inch screw bolts to each rail, and great attention must be given to the rail joints, which must be secured by angle fish plates, with six bolts.

40. The railway must be equipped with the most approved system of signals, to guard against accidents; and there shall be the necessary telegraph and signal devices.

41. Stations shall be arranged as specified on the map of line as follows:

STATIONS ON ROUTE NO. I.

The first station shall be at or near the intersection of Myrtle avenue and Kent avenue.

The second station shall be at or near the intersection of Flushing avenue and Kent avenue.

The third station shall be at or near the intersection of Clymer street and Kent avenue.

The fourth station shall be at or near the intersection of Broadway and Kent avenue.

The fifth station shall be at or near the intersection of Grand street and Kent avenue.

The sixth station shall be at or near the intersection of North Ninth street and Kent avenue.

The seventh station shall be at or near the intersection of Greenpoint avenue and Franklin street.

The eighth station shall be at or near the intersection of Green street and Franklin street.

The ninth station shall be at or near the intersection of Manhattan avenue and Commercial street.

STATIONS ON ROUTE NO. II.

The first station shall be at or near the intersection of the Elevated Road with Atlantic avenue.

The second station shall be at or near the intersection of New Jersey avenue and Eastern Parkway.

The third station shall be at or near the intersection of the Eastern Parkway and Washington street.

The fourth station shall be at or near the intersection of the Eastern Parkway and Montauk avenue.

The fifth station shall be at or near the intersection of Glenmore avenue and Market street.

The sixth station shall be at or near the intersection of Grant avenue and Liberty avenue.

And they shall be convenient of access from the street or the intersecting cross streets.

42. The platforms of stations shall be on a level with the platforms of the cars, and shall be capable of sustaining a load of eighty pounds per square foot.

43. Each station shall have ample space under cover to accommodate passengers waiting for trains.

44. The stairs, stringers, and all parts of the stations, except the platform, doors, windows, inside sheathing, and whatever is necessary to be of wood, shall be of iron, properly galvanized.

45. All station platforms and stairs shall be protected by a substantial iron railing.

46. All axles shall be of steel of ample size, and all wheels in use under rolling stock shall have steel tires—all to be of the best modern construction, and the tires shall be turned on the tread.

47. All trains shall be provided with devices adequate to prevent ashes, grease, or water from falling into the street.

48 At every station suitable pans shall be provided to catch all drip from the engines when standing; these pans to be water tight with outlets to the gutters.

49. All car axles shall be provided with the best devices used in railway practice to catch the axles and prevent them from getting adrift in case of fracture.

50. Authority is given for construction of the necessary turnouts, switches, sidings, connections, landing places, the stations hereinbefore named, platforms, stairways, elevators, telegraph and signal devices, and such other requisite appliances upon the route or routes determined by the Commissioners as shall be proper for the construction of the railways proposed.

51. All the materials used in the construction of the work shall be of the best quality, and the work shall be executed in the best style in a workmanlike manner and be equal to the best and most modern construction.

52. It is the intention and spirit of these specifications to provide in every respect for a first class structure, and no omissions of specific requirements to this effect, if any exist, shall in any case be construed in any way to invalidate this general requirement.

53. All work shall be done on the streets or below the surface subject to the inspection and under the rules and regulations of the Department of City Works. All foundation plans that conflict with the sewers, water pipes, or street basins now built shall be submitted and approved by the Department, and all the necessary change to be made to prevent damage to the existing sewers, street basins or water pipes shall be done under the supervision and instruction of the Engineer of the Department.

54. No cars or engines shall be cleaned or washed on or over a public street or place, and ashes and refuse matter shall not at any time be dumped or deposited or allowed to fall on any public street or place.

55. These specifications shall be incorporated into and shall constitute an essential part of every contract made by the Company for materials or construction.

Approved May 7th, 1888.

By order of the Board.

GEORGE W. BROWN,
Secretary.

SAMUEL R. PROBASCO,
Engineer to Com.

On motion of Commissioner Brown the following resolution was unanimously adopted :

Resolved, That the time within which the portions of the railway or railways for which routes have been heretofore fixed, determined and located by these Commissioners, shall be constructed and ready for operation, is hereby fixed and determined as follows :

ROUTE No. I.

First—The portion of the railway or railways to be constructed from Myrtle avenue to Grand street, one year from July 1, 1888.

Second—The portion of the railway or railways to be constructed from Grand street to Greenpoint avenue, two years from July 1, 1888.

Third—The portion of the railway or railways to be constructed from Greenpoint avenue to end of route at Newtown Creek, three years from July 1, 1888.

ROUTE No. II.

First—The portion of the railway or railways to be constructed from the old City Line to New Jersey avenue. one year from July 1, 1888.

Second—The portion of the railway or railways to be constructed from New Jersey avenue to Montauk avenue, three years from July 1, 1888.

Third—The portion of the railway or railways to be constructed from Montauk avenue to City Line, five years from July 1, 1888.

On motion of Commissioner Almy, the following resolution was unanimously adopted:

Resolved—That each of the periods and limitations of time hereinbefore fixed and determined as the time within which the several sections or portions of railway or railways shall be constructed and ready for operation is, however, subject to this proviso as follows: That the time unavoidably consumed in obtaining the consents of property owners and local authorities required by the Constitution and Laws of the State of New York, or by the pendency of legal proceedings, shall not be deemed a part of any period of time within which the construction and completion of such railway or railways, or any section, sections, portion or portions thereof are required to be made; but the time, if any, during which such unavoidable delay shall continue, shall be added to each of the periods hereby otherwise limited for construction and completion of the said railway or railways, or any section, sections, portion or portions thereof.

On motion of Commissioner Doherty the following resolution was unanimously adopted:

Resolved, That the rates of fare authorized and allowed to be charged and collected upon trains to be run upon such railway or railways or upon any portion or part thereof, shall be five cents for each passenger, the same being the rate of fare by this Board of Commissioners fixed and determined as the maximum rate to be paid for transportation and conveyance of passengers over such railway or railways.

On motion of Commissioner Brown the following resolution was unanimously adopted.

Resolved, That the amount of the capital stock of the Company to be formed for the purpose of constructing, maintaining and operating such railway or railways shall be three hundred thousand (300,000) dollars, divided into three thousand (3,000) shares of the par value of One hundred (100) dollars each, subject to the right to increase the capital stock from time to time as authorized by law. On subscribing each subscriber is required to pay in cash five (5) per centum of the par value of the number of shares subscribed for by him.

Adjourned to Thursday, May 10, 1888, at 9 A. M.

GEORGE W. BROWN,
Secretary.

COMMISSIONERS OF RAPID TRANSIT,
City of Brooklyn,
Room No. 6, Hall of Records,
Thursday, May 10th, 1888, 9 A. M.

The Board met pursuant to adjournment.

Present—Commissioners George W. Almy, George W. Brown and Eugene Doherty.

Commissioner Almy was elected temporary Chairman.

The minutes of the last meeting were read and action upon them was deferred.

Upon motion of Commissioner Brown it was

Resolved, That a copy of the specifications be attached to and form a part of the map.

On motion of Commissioner Brown,

Resolved, That in addition to the stations mentioned in Section 41, of the general plans and specifications the Company may construct such intermediate stations as the demands of traffic may require.

Adjourned to Monday, May 14, 9 A. M.

GEORGE W. BROWN,
Secretary.

COMMISSIONERS OF RAPID TRANSIT,
City of Brooklyn,
Room No. 6, Hall of Records.
Brooklyn May 14, 1888, 9 A. M.

The Board met pursuant to adjournment.

Present—Commissioners Thomas S. Moore, George W. Almy, George W. Brown, Thomas H. McGrath and the Engineer.

The minutes of the 10th and 14th insts. were read and approved.

There was general discussion relative to plans and organization.

Adjourned to Thursday, May 17, 1888, at 9 A. M.

GEORGE W. BROWN,
Secretary.

COMMISSIONERS OF RAPID TRANSIT,
City of Brooklyn,
Room No. 6, Hall of Records,
Thursday, May 17, 1888, 9 A. M.

The Board met pursuant to adjournment.

Present—Commissioners George W. Almy, George W. Brown and the Engineer.

There being no quorum present, the meeting was adjourned to Monday, May 21, 1888, at 5 P. M.

GEORGE W. BROWN,
Secretary.

COMMISSIONERS OF RAPID TRANSIT,
City of Brooklyn,
Room No. 6, Hall of Records,
Monday, May 21, 1888, 5 P. M.

The Board met pursuant to adjournment.

Present—Commissioners Thomas S. Moore, George W. Almy, George W. Brown and Eugene Doherty.

Reading of the minutes was dispensed with.

There was discussion relative to organization.

Adjourned to Wednesday, May 23, 1888, at 5 P. M.

GEORGE W. BROWN,
Secretary.

COMMISSIONERS OF RAPID TRANSIT,
City of Brooklyn,
Room No. 6, Hall of Records,
Wednesday, May 23, 1888, 5 P. M.

The Board met pursuant to adjournment.

Present—Commissioners Thomas S. Moore, George W. Almy, George W. Brown and Eugene Doherty.

Reading of minutes was dispensed with.

There was discussion as to Articles of Association and other matters of business connected with the Commission.

Adjourned to Friday, May 25, 1888, at 5. P. M.

GEORGE W. BROWN,
Secretary.

85

COMMISSIONERS OF RAPID TRANSIT,
City of Brooklyn,
Room No. 6, Hall of Records,
Friday, May 25th, 1888, 5 P. M.

The Board met pursuant to adjournment.

Present—All the Commissioners.

The minutes of the 14th, 21st and 23d instants were read and approved.

On motion of Commissioner Brown, the following resolution was unanimously adopted:

Resolved, That the resolution passed April 14th, which reads as follows: "*Resolved*, That said corporation shall not be required to build or operate a railroad upon any portion of any route fixed by these Commissioners as aforesaid, upon which any other corporation duly authorized to do so shall have built or operated a railroad," be and the same is hereby rescinded.

There was lengthy discussion upon business connected with the Commission.

Adjourned to Thursday, May 31, at 10 A. M.

GEORGE W. BROWN,
Secretary.

COMMISSIONERS OF RAPID TRANSIT,
City of Brooklyn,
Room No. 6, Hall of Records.
Thursday, May 31, 1888, 10 A. M.

The Board met pursuant to adjournment.

Present—Commissioners Thomas S. Moore, George W Almy, George W. Brown and Eugene Doherty.

The minutes of the meeting of the 25th instant were read and approved.

There was discussion as to the proposed Articles of Association.

Adjourned to Saturday, June 2d, 1888, at 9 A. M.

GEORGE W. BROWN,
Secretary.

COMMISSIONERS OF RAPID TRANSIT.
City of Brooklyn,
Room No. 6, Hall of Records,
Saturday, June 2, 1888, 9.30 A. M.

The Board met pursuant to adjournment.

Present—All the Commissioners.

On motion of Commissioner Brown the following resolution was unanimously adopted :

Resolved, That the following Articles of Association be, and they are hereby adopted by this Board of Commissioners as the Articles of Association for the Company to be formed by it, and which said Board of Commissioners are required by the statute to prepare :

Articles of Association for the "Fulton Elevated Railway Company," prepared pursuant to an act of the Legislature of the State of New York, entitled "An Act further to provide for the construction and operation of a steam railway or railways in the counties of the State," passed June eighteenth, in the year eighteen hundred and seventy five, and the Acts amendatory thereof, by the Commissioners appointed by the Mayor of the City of Brooklyn, on the fourth day of February, 1888, in compliance with the provisions of said Acts.

Article I.—The name of the Corporation hereby formed is "The Fulton Elevated Railway Company."

Article II.—The said corporation is formed for the purpose of constructing, maintaining and operating railways upon the routes hereinafter mentioned, fixed by said Commissioners, for public use in the conveyance of persons and property, and with the power and authority so to do, so far as such power can be developed thereon in or through Articles of Association prepared as aforesaid, and the proceedings of said Commission heretofore had and herein mentioned or referred to.

Said Corporation shall be subject to all the provisions and requirements of said acts of the Legislature, so far as such provisions and requirements are intended to be applicable to corporations formed under the authority thereof, and shall have all the rights, powers, franchises and privileges intended to be allowed to corporations formed under the authority thereof.

Article III.—The capital stock of the corporation shall be three hundred thousand dollars ($300,000), divided into three thousand (3,000) shares, of the par value of one hundred dollars each, subject, however, to the right to increase the capital stock from time to time as provided in and by said Acts.

Article IV.—The affairs of the Company shall be managed by a Board of nine Directors.

Article V.—The Company is to be continued for ninety-nine years, from the first day of June, 1888.

ARTICLE VI.—The several condition, requirements, and particulars by said Commissioners determined, pursuant to Section 4 of said Act of the Legislature and the Acts amendatory thereof, (and which are shown in the resolutions hereinafter in this article set forth), are hereby set forth and embodied as component parts of these Articles of Association.

(a) One of the resolutions in this article referred to was duly adopted by said Commissioners at a meeting duly convened and held in the City of Brooklyn, on the twenty-seventh day of February, 1888, and is as follows:

Resolved, That these Commissioners hereby determine that there is a necessity in the City of Brooklyn of a steam railway or railways for the transportation of passengers, mails or freight, in addition to any heretofore authorized.

(b.) The following resolutions in this article hereinbefore referred to were duly adopted by said Board of Commissioners, at a meeting duly convened and held in the City of Brooklyn, on the fourteenth day of April, 1888, and are as follows:

Resolved, That in pursuance of the powers conferred upon us by Chapter 606 of the Laws of 1875, and the acts amendatory thereof, we, the Commissioners appointed by the Mayor of the City of Brooklyn, on the 4th day of February, 1888, do hereby fix and determine the route or routes of a steam railway or railways in the City of Brooklyn, as follows:

ROUTE I.

Beginning on and over Manhattan avenue, at or near its intersection with Newtown Creek; running thence over, through and along Manhattan avenue to Commercial street; thence over, through and along Commercial street to Franklin street; thence over, through and along Franklin street to Kent avenue; thence over, through and along Kent avenue to Myrtle avenue.

Resolved, That in pursuance of the powers conferred

upon us by Chapter 606 of the Laws of 1875, and the acts amendatory thereof, we, the Commissioners, appointed by the Mayor of the City of Brooklyn, on the 4th day of February, 1888, do hereby fix and determine the route or routes of a steam railway or railways in the City of Brooklyn, as follows:

Route II.

Beginning on and over Fulton street, at its intersection with the former boundary line, between the City of Brooklyn, and the Town of New Lots; thence over, through and along Fulton street to Jamaica avenue; thence over, through and along Jamaica avenue to any point on said avenue, East of Vesta avenue (formerly Van Sindaren avenue), and West of Williams place; thence over, through and across private property to and across Herkimer street; thence over, through and along Herkimer street to Williams place; thence over, through and along Williams place to, over and across East New York avenue and Atlantic avenue to Snedeker avenue; thence over, through and along Snedeker avenue to the Eastern Parkway; thence over, through and along the Eastern Parkway to Market street; thence over, through and along Market street to Liberty avenue; thence over, through and along Liberty avenue to the boundary line between the City of Brooklyn and the Town of Jamaica.

Provided that the Company authorized to build, or which may acquire the right to build a railway or railways upon said above described route, may build the same wholly upon said described route, or may vary the same as follows:

Beginning on and over Fulton street, at its intersection with the former boundary line between the City of Brooklyn and the Town of New Lots; running thence over, through and along Fulton street to Jamaica avenue; thence over, through and along Jamaica avenue to William's place; thence over, through and along William's place to, over and across East New York avenue and Atlantic avenue to Snedeker avenue; thence over, through and along Snedeker avenue to the Eastern Parkway; thence over, through and along the Eastern Parkway to Market street; thence over, through and along Market street to Liberty avenue; thence over, through and along Liberty avenue to the boundary line between the City of Brooklyn and the Town of Jamaica.

Or said company may vary said route as follows:

Beginning on and over Fulton street, at its intersection with the former boundary line between the City of Brooklyn and the Town of New Lots; running thence over, through and along Fulton street to Jamaica avenue; thence over, through and along Jamaica avenue to and across East New York avenue to Alabama avenue; thence over, through and along Alabama avenue to the Eastern Parkway; thence over, through and along the Eastern Parkway to Market street; thence over, through and along Market street to Liberty avenue; thence over, through and along Liberty avenue to the boundary line between the City of Brooklyn and the Town of Jamaica.

Resolved, That the location of the routes hereinabove designated, and of each thereof, shall, and does include the right to construct, use and operate in connection therewith, the usual necessary depots, stairways, tracks, sidings, turnouts, curves, switches, platforms and other appurtenances incidental to the construction, operation and maintenance of elevated railroads and to use and occupy the portions of the various streets under or adjacent to said road for that purpose.

Resolved, That whenever either of the routes hereinbefore fixed and determined, crosses any street, avenue, place or lands, such route includes and is intended to include such crossings and so much of said street, avenue, place or land as is there crossed as will allow and enable the construction of continuous connected lines of railway along routes so crossing.

Resolved, That whenever either of the routes hereinbefore fixed and determined is stated to commence, pass or end at the intersection of any street or avenue upon which a route or routes have been by this Commission fixed and determined, or upon which any elevated railroad has been constructed, or where any such route or routes commence, pass or terminate on the opposite side of any such street or avenue. Such route or routes shall be deemed to commence, pass or end, as the case may be, at the railway which shall be constructed on such street or avenue at which such route begins, passes or ends, so as to allow and permit of a connection between the railways projected or constructed on each of said intersecting streets or avenues, including such curves as may be necessary for that purpose.

ARTICLE VII.—The several conditions, requirements and particulars by said Commissioners heretofore determined, pursuant to Sections five and six of the said act of the Legislature, and which are shown in the resolutions hereinafter, in this article set forth, are hereby set forth and embodied as component parts of these Articles of Association.

(*a.*) The first of the resolutions in this article referred to was duly adopted by said Commissioners at a meeting duly convened and held in the City of Brooklyn, on the seventh day of May, 1888, and is as follows:

Resolved, That the Commissioners appointed by the Mayor of the City of Brooklyn, on the fourth day of February, 1888, under and in compliance with the provisions of Chapter 606 of the Laws of 1875, and the Act or Acts amendatory thereof, having by such public notice as they deemed most proper and effective, invited the submission of plans for the construction and operation of a railway or railways for the purpose provided for by said Acts, and having examined and considered the plans and devices submitted to them, do hereby select and decide upon plans for the construction for such railway or railways with the necessary supports, turnouts, switches, sidings, stations, buildings, platforms, telegraph and signal devices, and other requisite appliances upon the route or routes in the locations determined upon by them, by resolutions adopted on the fourteenth day of April, 1888, as follows:

First..—The plans as shown upon the maps herewith filed and marked, respectively, A, B, C, D, E and F, and signed by the Secretary and Engineer of the Commission.

Second.—The general plan of construction, as follows:

GENERAL PLAN AND SPECIFICATIONS FOR AN ELEVATED RAILWAY.

1. The general plan or plans of the structure shall be of an Elevated Railway, suported upon a row or rows of columns; the track or tracks shall be carried by longitudinal girders, resting either upon the tops of the columns or upon transverse girders supported by the columns.

2. Where the width of the street between the curbstones does not exceed forty feet, the plan of construction shall be as follows, to wit, with a row of columns on the line of each curb, and a superstructure carrying the tracks upon transverse girders spanning the street.

3. Where the width of the street or avenue between the curbstones is more than forty feet, the plan of construction shall be as follows, as the company constructing the railway shall elect, *i. e.*, either *First,* with a row of columns upon the line of each curb and a superstructure carrying the tracts upon transverse girders spanning the street; or, *Second,* with two rows of columns in the roadway of the street and a superstructure carrying the tracks either upon transverse girders or over each row of columns; but no columns authorized in this plan of construction shall be erected on any avenue or street except in the Twenty-sixth Ward and on the street or avenue known as Eastern Parkway.

4. Whenever a column or a row of columns is above authorized to be upon a line of curb, such columns or row of columns shall be erected only within the line of curbstones, and shall be there so situated and placed as not to obstruct vehicles or the ordinary trafic for travel of the roadway or street.

5. There shall not be more than two rows of columns or more than two tracks in any one street or avenue or public place, except as hereinafter authorized.

6. No columns shall be erected between any two tracks of street railroad, now upon the surface of the roadway of the street, except, as herein otherwise authorized.

7. Except where the width of a cross street, between the curbs thereof, is forty feet or more, every cross street shall be spanned by a single span, when and where the plan of construction used is one having a row of columns upon a curb line.

8. The transverse diameter of a column authorized to be in the roadway of any street shall not exceed eighteen inches at the base and thence for at least ten feet above the surface of the roadway; and the transverse diameter of a column authorized to be on the line of a curb, shall not exceed twenty-six inches at the base and thence for at least ten feet above the surface of the roadway.

9. When and where the plan of construction used is one having two rows of columns in the roadway of the street, no column shall be erected between the curb lines of a cross street, elsewhere than upon the centre line of such cross street, but may be there erected when the distance between curbs exceeds forty feet.

10. A single or double track may be placed between longitudinal girders and carried by iron floor beams, the latter supported by the longitudinal girders.

11. Where columns are authorized to be in the roadway on each side of a street railroad track upon the surface of the roadway the transverse distance between the columns shall be at least twenty-one feet in the clear.

12. Where two rows of columns are authorized, and either row is placed in the roadway of the street, the columns shall be erected in pairs, and both columns of each pair shall stand in line at right angles to the axis of the street, except on curves.

13. The transverse diameter of columns above indicated does not include fenders; and adequate fenders shall be fitted round the base of each column placed in the roadway to prevent the hubs of the wheels of passing vehicles from striking the columns.

14. The longitudinal distance between columns on the curb shall be at least twenty feet. The longitudinal distance between columns in the roadway shall be at least thirty-five feet except as herein otherwise provided.

15. On curves of three hundred feet radius or less, the longitudinal distance between the columns in the roadway may be reduced to not less than twenty-five feet.

16. No part of the girder or superstructure shall be less than fourteen feet above the level of the street.

17. Upon every track there shall be at least four continuous longitudinal stringers of sufficient size, of the best quality of yellow pine timber. The joints of such longitudinal stringers shall be scarfed and bolted, and such stringers shall be securely fastened to each alternate support on which they rest, so as to tie the structure firmly together and give it stiffness in a longitudinal direction, and also act as guard rails. This requirement may be fulfilled either by longitudinal stringers under the rail, or by safety guards of timber, if made to comply with the above conditions.

18. The materials used for that part of the structure above the ground shall be wrought iron or steel—except that the connections between the posts which form a cluster column may be of cast iron—and except the rails which shall be of steel—and except the ties supporting the rails which shall be of the best quality and kind of selected yellow pine timber. The safety guards, if of wood, shall be of

the best quality and kind of yellow pine timber. Wood shall not be placed in any position where it may not readily be removed without interrupting the travel on the road.

19. The structure may be built of lattice, or plate girders for the transverse girders, and of lattice girders modified by the use of plates in place of diagonals in the panels near the ends of the girders.

20. The wrought iron shall be of the following general character: Tough, fibrous and uniform in quality, having an elastic limit of 24,000 to 26,000 pounds, and an ultimate tensile strength of 48,000 to 50,000 pounds per square inch of section; under tensile strain it shall stretch from 10 to 15 per cent. in 8 inches.

21. All rivets shall be of double refined iron, which shall have an ultimate tensile strength of 60,000 pounds to the square inch. The rivet holes shall be truly and accurately opposite each other; and the rivets shall enter the holes without drifting or forcing, and shall fill the holes.

22. No part of the structure shall be subjected to a greater strain of tension or compression than 10,000 pounds to the square inch; and no part shall be subjected to a greater shearing strain than 7,500 pounds to the square inch; and the structure shall not be proportioned for a less moving load than 2,000 pounds per lineal foot for each track.

23. The maximum deflection of any girder under the passage of a train shall never exceed one fifteen hundredth ($\frac{1}{1500}$) of its length.

24. The angle bars and plates composing the longitudinal parts of a column or girder shall be in single pieces, except in the case of a girder of more than forty feet in length.

25. All parts which make up the section of a column except where cluster columns are used, shall be of equal thickness and uniform quality.

26. The strength of the column shall be proportioned by Gordon's formula for the ratio of the diameter to the length, with five as a factor of safety, or the equivalent thereof.

27. The different parts of the structure and their connections shall be properly proportioned to resist all the strains which the momentum of the train can, by the application of brakes, or in any other manner, impart to the structure.

28. The foundations for the columns shall consist of brick-work of the best quality, except where in water, when the best Rosendale cement concrete, in parts of one of sand to two of cement to five of broken stone shall be used until a sufficient height is reached above the water when brick-work shall be used.

29. All masonry for foundations shall measure at least three feet square upon the top, at least six feet square at the bottom ; shall not be less than seven feet six inches in depth below the curb. The base shall be a bed of concrete, six inches thick, so as to make a bed for the masonry not less than seven feet square. When the span is more than fifty feet, the dimensions of the foundations shall be larger proportionally.

30. The earth is to be prepared for this masonry by being made firm and solid, and covered with a bed of good hydraulic mortar not less than six inches in depth.

31. Every column or post shall be secured to the masonry by means of a heavy plate of cast iron, so proportioned as to distribute the weight which comes upon it uniformly over the foundation. This plate shall be fastened by sufficiently strong, wrought iron bolts, one and a half inches in diameter—not less than four feet six inches long—the bolts having heads which shall be upset and not welded, and having cast iron socket washers of sufficient size, not less than twelve inches square, built in the masonry. The cast iron plate, its connections with the columns, the wrought iron bolts, and their heads and washers, shall possess sufficient strength to receive and

resist equally well with the column all strains which may come upon the latter The castings shall be of good, tough iron, and before setting shall be thoroughly examined to discover any flaws or imperfections.

32. All the iron work beneath the surface of the street shall be cleaned from rust and scale, and well covered with coal tar varnish before it is set.

33. Good hydraulic cement mortar shall be used in the masonry, of the usual proportions of two parts of sand to one of cement, and fresh burned Rosendale cement of the first quality shall be used in all cases. The bricks shall be hard burned Haverstraw and of the best quality.

34. The foundations, where necessary, shall be increased, in area, so that in no case shall a weight greater than two thousand pounds to the square foot come upon any base.

35. All wrought iron work shall receive, before being riveted together a coat of thick linseed oil and red lead on all surfaces in contact, so that the spaces inclosed shall be completely filled, and shall receive one coat of boiled oil, well brushed on and dried before leaving the shop, and after erection shall receive such covering of paint as to protect all parts of the structure, which shall, where practicable, be accessible for the purpose of painting.

36. Efficient guard rails of iron or wood shall be provided, so that, in case of accident, the cars shall be effectually prevented from leaving the structure.

37. Continuous brakes (either vacuum or pressure), so arrranged as to be under the control of the engineer, shall be applied to all trains, and to every car in each train, as well as efficient hand brakes.

38. All switches shall be split switches of the most approved design, so that if left open or placed wrong, the main track shall not be broken. or offer any impediment which may cause the derailment of a passing train.

39. Rails shall be of steel, not less in weight than fifty-six pounds per lineal yard. They shall be laid and

fastened in the most approved manner on cross-ties, 7 inches by 9 inches, laid not over two feet between centres and, when borne by continuous stringers, in addition to the ordinary rail spikes, shall have six three-quarter inch screw bolts to each rail, and great attention must be given to the rail joints, which must be secured by angle fish plates, with six bolts.

40. The railway must be equipped with the most approved system of signals, to guard against accidents; and there shall be the necessary telegraph and signal devices.

41. Stations shall be arranged as specified on the map of line as follows:

STATIONS ON ROUTE NO. I.

The first station shall be at or near the intersection of Myrtle avenue and Kent avenue.

The second station shall be at or near the intersection of Flushing avenue and Kent avenue.

The third station shall be at or near the intersection of Clymer street and Kent avenue.

The fourth station shall be at or near the intersection of Broadway and Kent avenue.

The fifth station shall be at or near the intersection of Grand street and Kent avenue.

The sixth station shall be at or near the intersection of North Ninth street and Kent avenue.

The seventh station shall be at or near the intersection of Greenpoint avenue and Franklin street.

The eighth station shall be at or near the intersection of Green street and Franklin street.

The ninth station shall be at or near the intersection of Manhattan avenue and Commercial street.

STATIONS ON ROUTE NO. II.

The first station shall be at or near the intersection of the Elevated Road with Atlantic avenue.

The second station shall be at or near the intersection of New Jersey avenue and Eastern Parkway.

The third station shall be at or near the intersection of the Eastern Parkway and Washington street.

The fourth station shall be at or near the intersection of the Eastern Parkway and Montauk avenue.

The fifth station shall be at or near the intersection of Glenmore avenue and Market street.

The sixth station shall be at or near the intersection of Grant avenue and Liberty avenue.

And they shall be convenient of access from the street or the intersecting cross streets.

42. The platforms of stations shall be on a level with the platforms of the cars, and shall be capable of sustaining a load of eighty pounds per square foot.

43. Each station shall have ample space under cover to accommodate passengers waiting for trains.

44. The stairs, stringers, and all parts of the stations, except the platform, doors, windows, inside sheathing, and whatever is necessary to be of wood, shall be of iron, properly galvanized.

45. All station platforms and stairs shall be protected by a substantial iron railing.

46. All axles shall be of steel of ample size, and all wheels in use under rolling stock shall have steel tires—all to be of the best modern construction, and the tires shall be turned on the tread.

47. All trains shall be provided with devices adequate to prevent ashes, grease, or water from falling into the street.

48. At every station suitable pans shall be provided to catch all drip from the engines when standing; these pans to be water tight with outlets to the gutters.

49. All car axles shall be provided with the best devices used in railway practice to catch the axles and prevent them from getting adrift in case of fracture.

50. Authority is given for construction of the necessary turnouts, switches, sidings, connections, landing places, the stations hereinbefore named, platforms, stairways, elevators. telegraph and signal devices, and such other requisite appliances upon the route or routes determined by the Commissioners as shall be proper for the construction of the railways proposed.

51. All the materials used in the construction of the work shall be of the best quality, and the work shall be executed in the best style in a workmanlike manner and be equal to the best and most modern construction.

52. It is the intention and spirit of these specifications to provide in every respect for a first class structure, and no omissions of specific requirements to this effect, if any exist, shall in any case be construed in any way to invalidate this general requirement.

53. All work shall be done on the streets or below the surface subject to the inspection and under the rules and regulations of the Department of City Works. All foundation plans that conflict with the sewers, water pipes, or street basins now built shall be submitted and approved by the Department, and all the necessary changes to be made to prevent damage to the existing sewers, street basins or water pipes shall be done under the supervision and instruction of the Engineer of the Department.

54. No cars or engines shall be cleaned or washed on or over a public street or place, and ashes and refuse matter shall not at any time be dumped or deposited or allowed to fall on any public street or place.

55. These specifications shall be incorporated into and shall constitute an essential part of every contract made by the Company for materials or construction.

(*b*). The following resolutions in this article hereinbefore referred to were duly adopted by the said Board of Commissioners at the same meeting on the said seventh day of

May, 1888. The said resolution were in words and figures following:—

Resolved, That the time within which the portions of the railway or railways for which routes have been heretofore fixed, determined and located by these Commissioners, shall be constructed and ready for operation, is hereby fixed and determined as follows:

ROUTE No. I.

First—The portion of the railway or railways to be constructed from Myrtle avenue to Grand street, one year from July 1, 1888.

Second—The portion of the railway or railways to be constructed from Grand street to Greenpoint avenue, two years from July 1, 1888.

Third—The portion of the railway or railways to be constructed from Greenpoint avenue to end of route at Newtown Creek, three years from July 1, 1888.

ROUTE No. II.

First—The portion of the railway or railways to be constructed from the old City Line to New Jersey avenue. one year from July 1, 1888.

Second—The portion of the railway or railways to be constructed from New Jersey avenue to Montauk avenue, three years from July 1, 1888.

Third—The portion of the railway or railways to be constructed from Montauk avenue to City Line, five years from July 1, 1888.

Resolved, That each of the periods and limitations of time hereinbefore fixed and determined as the time within which the several sections or portions of railway or railways shall be constructed and ready for operation is, however, subject to this proviso as follows: That the time unavoidably consumed in obtaining consents of property owners and local authorities required by the Constitution and Laws of the State of New York, or by the pendency of legal proceedings, shall not be deemed a part of any period of time within which the construction and completion of such railway or railways, or any section, sections, portion or portions thereof are required to be made; but the time, if any, during which such unavoidable delay shall continue, shall be added to each of the periods hereby otherwise limited for the construction and completion of the said railway or railways, or any section, sections, portion or portions thereof.

Resolved, That the rates of fare authorized and allowed to be charged and collected upon trains to be run upon such railway or railways or upon any portion or part thereof, shall be five cents, for each passenger, the same being the rate of fare by this Board of Commissioners fixed and determined as the maxium rate to be paid for transportation and conveyance of passengers over such railway or railways.

Resolved, That the amount of the capital stock of the company to be formed for the purpose of constructing, maintaining and operating such railway or railways shall be three hundred thousand (300,000) dollars, divided into three thousand (3,000) shares of the par value of one hundred (100) dollars each, subject to the right to increase the capital stock from time to time as authorized by law.

On subscribing, each subscriber is required to pay in cash, five (5) per centum of the par value of the number of shares subscribed for by him.

ARTICLE VIII.—In case such railway or railways or any of them shall not be completed within the time and upon the conditions hereinbefore and as to such portions provided, all rights and franchises acquired by such corporation shall be released and forfeited to the Supervisors of the County of Kings.

ARTICLE IX.—The persons who shall be entitled to receive the stock of said corporation shall be the corporators thereof, and no persons shall be entitled to receive any stock of said corporation, under the subscription to be made therefor as hereinbefore provided, pursuant to said acts of the legislature, unless at the time of subscribing therefor he shall subscribe his name to the agreement following, in person or by proxy, and with such signature indicate and state, in proper form, his residence and the number of shares subscribed for by him, and said agreement, with the signatures thereto, shall form and be a part of these Articles of Association; and no person shall sign such Articles of Association as a party thereto and corporator thereunder until he shall have made a proper subscription for stock of said company, as provided by the said Commissioners, and paid the Treasurer of such Commissioners the sum of five per centum thereon. In case any person who shall sign such agreement shall not become entitled to receive any stock of said corporation, his signature to such agreement shall be of no effect.

ARTICLE X.—The agreement above referred to is the following:—

We, the undersigned, who have each and severally subscribed for certain shares of the stock of said Corporation as shown opposite our respective names. and paid five per centum of the amount of such subscription as hereinbefore provided, hereby associate ourselves (with others, if any, who may be or become entitled to sign this agreement) for the purpose of forming a corporation, under the Articles of Association hereinbefore written, and each and severally assent to and agree to be bound by all the requirements of the same.

Dated Brooklyn, 1888.

NAME OF SUBSCRIBER.	RESIDENCE.	NUMBER OF SHARES SUBSCRIBED FOR.

On motion of Commissioner Brown, the following resolution was unanimously adopted:

Resolved, That a book of subscriptions to the capital stock of the Fulton Elevated Railway Company, of Brooklyn, be opened by this Board at the banking office of the Long Island Loan and Trust Company, No. 203 Montague street, in the City of Brooklyn, County of Kings, on Thursday, the 7th of June, 1888, at 9 o'clock A. M., and that subscriptions be then and there received on the payment of the fixed percentage thereon.

On motion of Commissioner Brown, the following resolution was unanimously adopted:

Resolved, That public notice of the opening of such book of subscriptions be given by the Secretary of this Board by advertising the same in the Brooklyn *Eagle,* the *Citizen,* and the Brooklyn Daily *Times,* daily, commencing this day and ending on the 6th day of June, 1888, which notice this Board hereby determines to be due public notice.

On motion of Commissioner Brown, the following resolution was unanimously adopted:

Resolved, That the following form of advertisement is hereby approved:

OFFICE OF THE COMMISSIONERS OF RAPID TRANSIT,
Room No. 6, Hall of Records,
Fulton Street,
Brooklyn, June 2d, 1888.

Notice is hereby given that a book of subscriptions for the capital stock of the Fulton Elevated Railway Company will be opened by the Board of Rapid Transit Commissioners, appointed by the Mayor of the City of Brooklyn, on the 4th day of February, 1888, at the banking office of the Long Island Loan and Trust Company, No. 203 Montague street, in the City of Brooklyn, on June 7th, 1888, at 9 o'clock A. M., and that subscriptions will then and there be received on the payment of five per cent. thereon, that being the percentage fixed by said Commissioners.

(Signed)

THOMAS S. MOORE,
President.

GEORGE W. BROWN,
Secretary.

On motion of Commissioner Brown, the following resolution was unanimously adopted :

Resolved, That the following form of subscription be annexed to the Articles of Association :

THE FULTON ELEVATED RAILWAY COMPANY.

Form of subscriptions to the capital stock.

Each of us, the undersigned, hereby subscribes to the capital stock of the Fulton Elevated Railway Company, which is to be incorporated and organized under the provisions of Chapter 606 of the Laws of 1875, and the act or acts amendatory thereof, with and according to the Articles of Association heretofore prepared (a copy of which is hereto annexed), in compliance with the requirements of said Acts, by the Commissioners, appointed by the Mayor of the City of Brooklyn, in the month of February, 1888, pursuant to the provisions thereof.

Each of us hereby promises, covenants and agrees to and with each other subscriber hereto, each for and in consideration of the promise, covenant and agreement of such other, and to and with the said Commissioners, each for and in consideration of such distribution of shares as may by him by said Commissioners be made, to take and pay for the number of shares hereinbelow by him written opposite to his name of the capital stock of said Company.

Each of us now pays in cash, on subscribing for such shares, five per centum of the par value of the number of shares by him hereinbelow written opposite to his name; and each of us hereby, for and upon such considerations, agrees that the remainder of the amount of the par value of such shares as may by the said Commissioners be allotted to him, shall be paid promptly and upon demand, in installments, as and whenever the Board of Directors of the Company shall, from time to time assess and call for the same.

And each of us who shall become a stockholder in said Corporation, for himself agrees, in consideration of the premises, to be bound by the said Articles of Association; and each of us hereby authorizes and empowers the persons, or any one or more of them who shall, pursuant to said acts, be elected to be the Directors for the first year of said corporation, in his behalf, to subscribe said Articles of Association.

Dated Brooklyn, June 7th, 1888.

On motion of Commissioner Almy the Board adjourned to Wednesday, June 6th, 1888, at 10 A. M.

GEORGE W. BROWN,
Secretary.

COMMISSIONERS OF RAPID TRANSIT,
City of Brooklyn,
Room No. 6, Hall of Records,
Wednesday, June 6, 1888, 9 A. M.

The Board met pursuant to adjournment.

Present—Commissioners Thomas S. Moore, George W. Almy, George W. Brown, and Eugene Doherty.

The minutes of the meeting of the 2d inst were read and approved.

The Secretary reported that he had ordered the notice of the meeting for the opening of the book of subscription to the capital stock of the Fulton Elevated Railway Company to be published in *The Brooklyn Daily Eagle*, *The*

Citizen and *The Brooklyn Daily Times,* daily for five days, commencing June 2, 1888.

Adjourned to June 7, at 9 A. M., at the office of the Long Island Loan and Trust Co.

GEORGE W. BROWN,
Secretary.

COMMISSIONERS OF RAPID TRANSIT,
Office of The Long Island Loan and Trust Co.,
201 Montague Street, Brooklyn, N. Y.
Thursday, June 7, 1888, 9 A. M

The Board met pursuant to adjournment.

Present—Commissioners Thomas S. Moore, George W. Almy, George W. Brown, and Eugene Doherty.

The reading of the minutes was dispensed with.

The Secretary produced advertisements giving public notice of the meeting this day, and of the opening of books of subscription for the capital stock of the Fulton Elevated Railway Company, as directed by resolution of the Board passed June 2d, inst.

Said advertisements and proofs are as follows:

STATE OF NEW YORK, }
  City of Brooklyn, } *ss:*

HERBERT PAYNE, of the City of Brooklyn in the County of Kings being duly sworn says that he is foreman of the publisher of *The Citizen*, a daily newspaper published in the City of Brooklyn, in the County of Kings aforesaid, and that the notice of which the annexed is a true copy has been published in said newspaper for five days successively, commencing on the second day of June, 1888.

HERBERT PAYNE.

Sworn and subscribed to this 7th day of June, 1888, before me.

P. F. McLaughlin,
Commissioner of Deeds,
City of Brooklyn.

Office of Commissioners of Rapid Transit,
Room No. 6, Hall of Records,
Fulton Street, Brooklyn, N. Y.,
June 2, 1888.

Notice is hereby given that a book of subscriptions for the capital stock of the Fulton Elevated Railway Company will be opened by the Board of Rapid Transit Commissioners appointed by the Mayor of the City of Brooklyn on the 4th day of February, 1888, at the banking office of The Long Island Loan and Trust Company, 203 Montague Street, in the City of Brooklyn, on June 7, 1888, at 9 o'clock A.M., and that subscriptions will then and there be received on the payment of five per cent. thereon, being the percentage fixed by the said Commissioners.

THOMAS S. MOORE,
President.

GEORGE W. BROWN,
Secretary.

State of New York, } ss.:
City of Brooklyn.

William H. Sutton, of the City of Brooklyn, in the County of Kings, being duly sworn says that he is foreman of the publisher of *The Brooklyn Daily Eagle*, a daily newspaper published in the City of Brooklyn in the County of Kings aforesaid, and that the notice of which the annexed is a true copy has been published in said newspaper for five days successively, commencing on the second day of June, 1888.

WM. H. SUTTON.

Sworn and subscribed to this 11th
day of June, 1888; before me,

JACOB G. CARPENTER,
Notary Public,
Kings County.

OFFICE OF COMMISSIONERS OF RAPID TRANSIT,
Room No. 6, Hall of Records.
Fulton Street, Brooklyn,
June 2, 1888.

Notice is hereby given that a book of subscriptions for the capital stock of the Fulton Elevated Railway Company will be opened by the Board of Rapid Transit Commissioners appointed by the Mayor of the City of Brooklyn, on the 4th day of February, 1888, at the banking office of the Long Island Loan and Trust Company, No. 203 Montague Street, in the City of Brooklyn, on June 7, 1888, at 9 o'clock A.M., and that subscriptions will be then and there received on the payment of five per cent. thereon, being the percentage fixed by the said Commissioners.

THOMAS S. MOORE,
President.

GEORGE W. BROWN,
Secretary.

STATE OF NEW YORK,
County of Kings, } ss.:

W. H. HELMLE, of the City of Brooklyn, in the County of Kings, being duly sworn says that he is foreman of the publisher of the *Brooklyn Daily Times*, a daily newspaper printed and published in the City of Brooklyn, County of Kings aforesaid, and that the notice, of which the annexed is a true copy, has been published in said newspaper three days, commencing on the 4th day of June, 1888, and on the 5th and 6th days of June, 1888.

WM. H. HELMLE.

Sworn to this 7th day of }
June, 1888, before me. }

A. C. WATERMAN,
Notary Public,
Kings County, N. Y.

COMMISSIONERS OF RAPID TRANSIT,
Room No. 6, Hall of Records,
Fulton Street, Brooklyn,
June 2, 1888.

Notice is hereby given that a book of subscriptions for the capital stock of the Fulton Elevated Railway Company will be opened by the Board of Rapid Transit Commissioners, appointed by the Mayor of the City of Brooklyn, on the 4th day of February, 1888. at the Banking office of The Long Island Loan and Trust Company, 203 Montague street, in the City of Brooklyn, on June 7th, 1888, at 9 o'clock A. M., and that subscriptions will be then and there received on the payment of five per cent. thereon, being the percentage fixed by the said Commissioners.

THOMAS S. MOORE,
President.

GEORGE W. BROWN,
Secretary.

The Board then formally opened a book of subscriptions to the capital stock of the Fulton Elevated Railway Company, and also the Articles of Association thereof heretofore adopted by this Board, and began receiving such subscriptions and the percentage to be paid thereon.

The book of subscription and printed form of the Articles of Association having been for some time opened for subscriptions, the following subscribers to the number of twenty-six made their respective subscriptions to the capital stock, amounting in the aggregate to three thousand (3,000) shares of One hundred dollars ($100) each, and paid five (5) per cent of the par value thereof, viz.: Fifteen thousand dollars ($15,000) in cash into the hands of the Treasurer of the Board of Rapid Transit Commissioners, as follows:

Name of Subscriber.	Residence.	No. of shares subscribed for.
James Jourdan,	174 Cumberland St., Brooklyn, N.Y.,	620
James H. Frothingham,	29½ So. Portland Ave., Brooklyn, N.Y.,	275
James H. Frothingham, Trustee,	" " "	75
James O. Sheldon, by		
James H. Frothingham, Att'y,	New York City,	156
Edward A. Abbott, by		
James Jourdan, Att'y,	Boston, Mass.,	300
Harvey Farrington, by		
James Jourdan, Att'y,	Brooklyn, N. Y.,	75
Wendell Goodwin,	New York City,	150
S. Newton Smith, by		
Wendell Goodwin, Att'y,	New York City,	75
Henry J. Robinson, by		
Wendell Goodwin, Att'y.	New York City,	150
Wm. H. Dunbar, by		
Wendell Goodwin, Att'y,	South Abington Station, Mass.,	150
Henry J. Davison, by		
Wendell Goodwin, Att'y,	New York City,	150
Charles P. Hemenway, by		
Wendell Goodwin, Att'y,	Boston, Mass.,	75
T. Quincey Browne, by		
Wendell Goodwin, Att'y,	Boston, Mass.,	75
Augustus Richardson, by		
Wendell Goodwin, Att'y,	Roxbury, Mass.,	75
Frederick D. Hussey, by,		
Wendell Goodwin, Att'y,	Hingham, Mass.,	75
Lewis Downing, Jr., by		
Wendell Goodwin, Att'y,	Concord, Mass.,	75
James H. Jourdan, by		
Wendell Goodwin, Att'y,	Brooklyn, N. Y.,	5
Willis A. Bardwell,	Brooklyn, N. Y.,	10
Theodore L. Frothingham, by		
Wendell Goodwin, Att'y,	Brooklyn, N. Y.,	10
George W. Chauncey, by		
Wendell Goodwin, Att'y,	Brooklyn, N. Y.,	30

Name of Subscriber.	Residence.	No. of shares subscribed for.
John Wallace, by Wendell Goodwin, Att'y,	New York City.	24
Edward R. Jourdan, by Wendell Goodwin, Att'y,	Brooklyn, N. Y.,	10
Andrew Bryson, Jr., by Wendell Goodwin, Att'y,	Brooklyn, N. Y.,	5
Joseph Strachan, by Wendell Goodwin, Att'y,	Brooklyn, N. Y.,	5
Frank F. Jones, by Wendell Goodwin, Att'y,	Brooklyn, N. Y.,	30
Walter K. Rossiter,	Brooklyn, N. Y.,	5
James Jourdan,	Brooklyn, N. Y.,	215

The following persons subscribed said subscription list and Articles of Association in person in the presence of the Commissioners:

James Jourdan, James H. Frothingham,
James H. Frothingham, Trustee. Wendell Goodwin,
Willis A. Bardwell, Walter K. Rossiter.

The following persons subscribed said subscription list and said Articles of Association by James Jourdan, their Attorney, who, at the time of subscribing, delivered to the Commissioners a power of attorney from each of said subscribers duly executed by said subscribers respectively, and in the following form:

Know all men by these presents, that I,
              of   in the State of
have made, constituted and appointed, and by these presents do make, constitute and appoint James Jourdan and James H. Frothingham, of the City of Brooklyn, in the State of New York, and Wendell Goodwin, of the City of New York, and each or either of them my true and lawful attorney, for me and in my name, place and stead, to subscribe for   shares of the capital stock of the Fulton Elevated Railway Company, of the par value of $100 each share, and to subscribe to the Articles of Association of said Company (as the same under the authority and power given by Chapter 606 of the Laws of 1875, and

the act or acts amendatory thereof, are prepared and fixed by the Commissioners appointed in the month of February, 1888, by the Mayor of the City of Brooklyn, under the provisions of said act), hereby giving and granting unto my said attorney full power and authority to do and perform all and every act and thing whatsoever to be done in and about the premises, or necessary or proper to make me a subscriber for, and entitled to obtain and have from said Company the stock aforesaid, as fully, to all intents and purposes, as I might or could do, if personally present and acting in that behalf.

In witness whereof I have hereunto set my hand and seal this day of in the year one thousand eight hundred and eighty-eight.

Sealed and delivered in the presence of

EDWARD A. ABBOTT.   HARVEY FARRINGTON.

The following person subscribed said subscription list and said Articles of Association by James H. Frothingham, his attorney, who at the time of subscribing delivered to the Commissioners a power of attorney from the subscriber duly executed by said subscriber, and in the form above set forth.   James O. Sheldon

The following persons subscribed said subscription list and said Articles of Association by Wendell Goodwin, their attorney, who, at the time of subscribing delivered to the Commissioners a power of attorney from each of said subscribers, duly executed by said subscribers respectively, and in the form above set forth.

S. Newton Smith,   Henry J. Robinson,
William H. Dunbar,   Henry J. Davison,
Charles P. Hemmenway,   T. Quincey Browne,
Augustus Richardson,   Frederick D. Hussey,
Lewis Downing, Jr.,   James H. Jourdan,
Theodore L. Frothingham,   George W. Chauncey,
John Wallace,   Edward R. Jourdan,
Andrew Bryson, Jr.,   Joseph Strachan,
            Frank F. Jones.

The Treasurer reported that he had deposited the sum of Fifteen thousand dollars ($15,000) received by him to his credit as Treasurer of the Commission, in The Long Island Loan and Trust Company.

On motion, the action of the Treasurer was unanimously approved.

Adjourned to Monday, June 11, 1888, at 9 A. M.

GEORGE W. BROWN,
Secretary.

COMMISSIONERS OF RAPID TRANSIT,
City of Brooklyn,
Room No. 6, Hall of Records,
Monday, June 11, 1888, 9 A. M.

The Board met pursuant to adjournment.

Present—Commissioners Thomas S. Moore, George W. Almy, George W. Brown, Thomas H. McGrath and Eugene Doherty.

The minutes of the meeting of the 6th and 7th insts. were read and approved.

On motion it was

Resolved, That the Secretary be and is hereby instructed to send notice to each of the subscribers to the Capital Stock of the Fulton Elevated Railway Company of a meeting for the election of Directors, to be held at this office, on Tuesday, the 26th inst., at 10 o'clock A. M.

Adjourned to Thursday, June 14, 1888, at 9 A. M.

GEORGE W. BROWN,
Secretary.

COMMISSIONERS OF RAPID TRANSIT,
City of Brooklyn,
Room No. 6, Hall of Records,
Thursday, June 14, 1888, 9 A. M.

The Board met pursuant to adjournment.

Present—Commissioners Thomas S. Moore, George W. Almy, George W. Brown, Thomas H. McGrath and Eugene Doherty.

The minutes of the meeting of the 11th inst. were read and approved.

The Secretary reported that he had caused a notice of a meeting for the election of directors to be served upon each subscriber to the capital stock of the Fulton Elevated Railway Company, of which the following is a copy:

OFFICE OF COMMISSIONERS OF RAPID TRANSIT,
City of Brooklyn,
Room No. 6. Hall of Records.
June 14, 1888.

Dear Sir:

The whole capital stock of the Fulton Elevated Railway Company having been subscribed for, and the percentage paid in, as prescribed by section 8 of Chapter 606, of the laws of 1875, you are hereby notified that the first meeting of the stockholders for organization and the election of nine Directors, will be held at the office of this Commission, Room 6, Hall of Records, City of Brooklyn, on the 26th day of June, 1888, at 10 o'clock A. M.

GEORGE W. BROWN,
Secretary.

On motion it was

Resolved, That Edward Murphy and Charles N. McGuire be and they are hereby appointed Inspectors of Election of the first election of Directors of the Fulton Elevated Railway Company, to be held by the subscribers for the stock therefor.

Adjourned to June 21, 1888, at 9.30 A. M.

GEORGE W. BROWN,
Secretary.

COMMISSIONERS OF RAPID TRANSIT,
City of Brooklyn,
Room No. 6, Hall of Records,
Thursday, June 21, 1888, 9.30 A. M.

The Board met pursuant to adjournment.

Present—Commissioners Thomas S. Moore, George W. Almy, George W. Brown, and Thomas H. McGrath.

Reading of the minutes was dispensed with.

There was discussion on matters of interest to the Board.

Adjourned to June 26, 1888, at 10 A. M.

GEORGE W. BROWN,
Secretary.

COMMISSIONERS OF RAPID TRANSIT,
City of Brooklyn,
Room No. 6, Hall of Records,
Tuesday, June 26, 1888, 10 A. M.

The Board met pursuant to adjournment.

Present—Commissioners Thomas S. Moore, George W. Almy, George W. Brown and Thomas H. McGrath.

The minutes of the meetings of the 21st and 24th insts. were read and approved.

The Secretary produced a copy of notice of this meeting for the election of Directors, with proof of service thereof, in accordance with resolution passed June 11th inst.

Said notice and proof are as follows:

CITY OF BROOKLYN, } ss.:
County of Kings,

GEORGE W. BROWN, being duly sworn, says that he is Secretary of the Rapid Transit Commission. That on the 14th day of June, 1888, he served a notice of which the annexed is a copy, upon the persons whose names are given below, by depositing a copy of such notice enclosed in a paper wrapper, the postage thereon being prepaid, in the general post office in the City of Brooklyn, addressed to each of said persons respectively as follows:

James Jourdan, 174 Cumberland st., Brooklyn, N. Y.
James H. Frothingham, 29½ South Portland ave., Brooklyn, N. Y.
James H. Frothingham, Trustee, 29½ South Portland ave., Brooklyn, N. Y.
James O. Sheldon, New York City.
Edward A. Abbott, Boston, Mass.
Harvey Farrington, Brooklyn, N. Y.
Wendell Goodwin, New York City.
S. Newton Smith, New York City.
Henry J. Robinson, New York City.
William H. Dunbar, South Abington Station, Mass.
Henry J. Davison, New York City.
Charles P. Hemmenway, Boston, Mass.
T. Quincey Browne, Boston, Mass.
Augustus Richardson, Roxbury, Mass.
Frederick D. Hussey, Hingham, Mass.
Lewis Downing, Jr., Concord, N. H.
James H. Jourdan, Brooklyn, N. Y.
Willis A. Bardwell, Brooklyn, N. Y.
Theodore L. Frothingham, Brooklyn, N. Y.

George W. Chauncey, Brooklyn, N. Y.
John Wallace, New York City.
Edward R. Jourdan, Brooklyn, N. Y.
Andrew Bryson, Jr., Brooklyn, N. Y.
Joseph Strachan, Brooklyn, N. Y.
Frank F. Jones, Brooklyn, N. Y.
Walter K. Rossiter, Brooklyn, N. Y.

GEORGE W. BROWN.

Sworn to before me this }
25th day of June, 1888.

THOMAS S. MOORE,
Notary Public,
Kings County.

OFFICE OF COMMISSIONERS OF RAPID TRANSIT,
City of Brooklyn,
Room 6, Hall of Records,
June 14th, 1888.

Dear Sir:

The whole capital stock of the Fulton Elevated Railway Company having been subscribed for, and the percentage paid in as prescribed by Section 8 of Chapter 606 of the Laws of 1875, you are hereby notified that the first meeting of the stockholders for organization and the election of nine Directors, will be held at the office of this Commission, Room 6, Hall of Records, City of Brooklyn, on the 26th day of June, 1888, at 10 o'clock A. M.

GEORGE W. BROWN,
Secretary.

Edward Murphy and Charles N. McGuire, who were elected at the meeting of June 14th to act as Inspectors of Election severally subscribed and took the following oath:

CITY OF BROOKLYN, } *ss.:*
County of Kings,

I, EDWARD MURPHY, of said city, do solemnly swear

that I will execute the duties of Inspector of the Election now to be held for Directors of the Fulton Elevated Railway Company, with strict impartiality and according to the best of my ability.

EDWARD MURPHY.

Sworn to before me this
26th day of June, 1888.

> THOMAS S. MOORE,
> Notary Public,
> Kings County.

CITY OF BROOKLYN, } ss.:
County of Kings,

I, CHARLES N. MCGUIRE, of said city, do solemnly swear that I will execute the duties of Inspector of Election now to be held for Directors of the Fulton Elevated Railway Company with strict impartiality and according to the best of my ability.

CHARLES N. McGUIRE.

Sworn to before me this
26th day of June, 1888.

> THOMAS S. MOORE,
> Notary Public,
> Kings County.

On motion of Commissioner Brown,

Resolved, That the polls be, and they are hereby declared open for the election of nine Directors of the Fulton Elevated Railway Company, and that they remain open one hour.

A power of attorney was then produced from stockholders not personally present, and whose stock was voted upon, of which the following is a copy:

I, one of the subscribers to the stock of the Fulton Elevated Railway Company have made, constituted and appointed, and by these presents do make, constitute and appoint James Jourdan and James H. Frothingham, of the City of Brooklyn, or either of them, my true and lawful attorney for me, and in my name, place and stead to act for me and in my name at the first election of the Directors for the said Fulton Elevated Railway Company, and in my name, place and stead to vote for Directors so to be elected, and to do any act or thing necessary to be done at such meeting, or at an adjourned meeting, in order to perfect the organization of said Company as fully to all intents and purposes as I might or could do if personally present, hereby ratifying and confirming all that my said attorney may lawfully do in and about the same.

     In witness whereof I have hereunto set my hand and seal this   day of 1888.

Signed in the presence of

Thereupon an election was duly held by the votes of 2,225 shares of stock being cast by fifteen stockholders present in person or represented by proxy.

At eleven o'clock the President declared the polls closed, and the Inspectors of Election thereupon made their certificate as follows:

OFFICE OF THE COMMISSIONERS OF RAPID TRANSIT,

City of Brooklyn,

Hall of Records,

Fulton Street.

We, the undersigned, being sworn and qualified as Inspectors for the election of the Directors for the Fulton Elevated Railway Company, do hereby certify that at an election held at this office on the 26th day of June, 1888, the total number of shares voting being Twenty-two hundred and fifty-five (2,255) the same being held by fifteen different subscribers to the stock of the said Company, the following named persons received the number of votes set opposite their respective names for Directors of the said Fulton Elevated Railway Company, viz:

James Jourdan,	2,255
James O. Sheldon,	2,255
Harvey Farrington,	2,255
S. Newton Smith,	2,255
Wendell Goodwin,	2,255
Henry J. Robinson,	2,255
James H. Frothingham,	2,255
Henry J. Davison,	2,255
Edward A. Abbot,	2,255

And the said Inspectors do therefore determine and declare that the following persons were at said election by the greatest number of votes duly elected as Directors of said Fulton Elevated Railway Company for the ensuing year, viz:

James Jourdan,	James O. Sheldon,
Harvey Farrington,	S. Newton Smith,
Wendell Goodwin,	Henry J. Robinson,
James H. Frothingham,	Henry J. Davison,

Edward A. Abbot.

In witness whereof we have hereunto subscribed our names in duplicate this 26th day of June, 1888.

EDWARD MURPHY,

CHARLES N. MCGUIRE.

The Secretary reported that he had made application for the printing of the minutes at the offices of the *Brooklyn Daily Eagle*, *The Brooklyn Daily Times* and *The Citizen*. The rates at the office of *The Citizen* being the lowest, viz: $1.00 per page for fifty copies, he had engaged it to do the work.

The Treasurer was authorized to pay to the Treasurer of the State of New York the organization tax on the capital stock of the Fulton Elevated Railway Company, to wit, the sum of $375.

Adjourned to Friday, June 29, 1888, at 9 30 A.M.

GEORGE W. BROWN,
Secretary.

COMMISSIONERS OF RAPID TRANSIT.
City of Brooklyn,
Room No. 6, Hall of Records,
Friday, June 29, 1888, 9.30 A. M.

The Board met pursuant to adjournment.

Present—Commissioners Thomas S. Moore, George W. Almy, George W. Brown and Thomas H. McGrath.

The minutes of the meeting of the 26th instant were read and approved.

The following bills were audited and allowed and the Treasurer was directed to pay them:

Edward Murphy, Inspector of Elections,	$ 10.00
Charles N. McGuire, Inspector of Elections,	10.00
Henry Hamilton, for carriage hire,	10.00
Thomas S. Moore, disbursements,	24.89
The N. Y. World, advertising,	132.40
Standard-Union, advertising,	10.50
The Citizen, advertising,	153.15
The Brooklyn Daily Times, advertising,	118.44
Samuel R. Probasco, for professional services as Engineer,	750.00

The Treasurer reported that he had made the payment of $375 to the State Treasurer as directed at the last meeting.

Adjourned to Monday, July 2, 1888, at 10 A. M.

GEORGE W. BROWN,
Secretary.

COMMISSIONERS OF RAPID TRANSIT,
City of Brooklyn,
Room No. 6, Hall of Records,
Monday, July 2, 1888, 10 A. M.

The Board met pursuant to adjournment.

Present—Commissioners Thomas S. Moore, George W. Almy, George W. Brown, Thomas H. McGrath and Eugene Doherty.

The minutes of the meetings of the 29th inst. were read and approved.

The following bills were audited and allowed and the Treasurer was directed to pay them.

George W. Brown, Disbursements, ... $12.00
Brooklyn Freie Presse, Advertising, . . . 75.00
Brooklyn Daily Eagle, Advertising, . . . 145.20
Mortimer B. O'Shea, Janitor, ... 50.00

The following communication was received from the Secretary of the Fulton Elevated Railway Company.

Brooklyn, N. Y., July 2, 1888.

To Thomas S. Moore, Esq.,
Pres. of the Board of Rapid Transit Commissioners:
Dear Sir:
I beg to advise you that a meeting of the Directors of the Fulton Elevated Railway Company, was held on

Saturday the 30th ult., pursuant to notice given by your Board, two-thirds of such Directors being present; that By-Laws were then unanimously adopted, a copy of which will be herewith enclosed for your information, and that an election of officers, in conformity therewith was duly had, the following persons being unanimously chosen, viz.:

 For President,   JAMES JOURDAN.
 For Vice-President,   WENDELL GOODWIN.
 For Treasurer,   JAMES H. FROTHINGHAM.
 For Secretary,   HENRY J. ROBINSON.

I beg further to say that a resolution was also adopted referring the adjustment of financial matters between your Board and the Company to the President of the Company with power.

    Yours, very respectfully,
      H. J. ROBINSON,
       Secretary.

On motion of Commissioner McGrath the following resolution was unanimously adopted:

Resolved, That this Commission tender to Honorable William H. Murtha, Register of Kings County, their thanks for the use of Room No. 6, Hall of Records Building, during the existence of the Commission, and also express their appreciation of many courtesies extended by him.

On motion of Commissioner Doherty the following resolution was unanimously adopted:

Resolved, That the Commissioners composing this Board appear before one of the Justices of the Supreme Court of this District, and verify under oath a certificate in duplicate setting forth the Articles of Association heretofore prepared by this Board, and the organization of the Fulton Elevated Railway Company of Brooklyn, for the purposes mentioned and provided for by law, and deliver the same to the Directors of said Company.

The Commissioners then proceeded in a body before the Honorable Edgar M. Cullen, Justice of the Supreme Court, at the Supreme Court Room, in the County Court House, and signed and verified the following certificate in duplicate:

CERTIFICATE OF ARTICLES OF ASSOCIATION,

and of the Organization of the

FULTON ELEVATED RAILWAY COMPANY,

made in compliance with the requirements of Section 9 of Chapter 606 of the Laws of 1875.

Brooklyn, July 2, 1888.

We, the undersigned, Thomas S. Moore, George W. Almy, George W. Brown, Thomas H. McGrath and Eugene Doherty, the Commissioners appointed by the Mayor of the City of Brooklyn, on February 4, 1888, under the authority conferred by an act of the Legislature of the State of New York, entitled "An Act further to provide for the construction and operation of a steam railway or railways in the Counties of this State," passed June 18, 1875, and the acts amendatory thereof and supplemental thereto, and by whom the Articles of Association of the Fulton Elevated Railway Company have been prepared, and under whose direction subscriptions thereto have been made, and the said Company been organized, do hereby, in pursuance of the provisions of law in such case made and provided, certify in duplicate as follows:

First—That the first twenty-four pages of paper hereto annexed correctly set forth the Articles of Association by us prepared for the said Fulton Elevated Railway Company.

Second—That said Company was organized as follows: Said Articles of Association having been duly prepared by said Board of Commissioners, and the different acts and proceedings mentioned or recited in the aforesaid Articles of Association having been first duly performed, or had, the said Board of Commissioners, after having given due public notice thereof, opened a book of subscriptions to the capital stock of said Company, at the office of the Long Island Loan and Trust Company, a banking office in the City of Brooklyn, County of Kings, on the 7th day of June, 1888, in the form shown in and by said Articles of Association and form of subscription hereto annexed. That, on the said day, subscriptions to the full amount of the capital stock of the said Company were made by twenty-six subscribers, who also subscribed to said Articles of Association as shown in and by the signatures appended to the said Articles of Association and form of subscription, and several papers granting and conferring powers of attorney, copies of which are hereto annexed, being then also delivered to the said Commissioners, all of whom were then present.

Third—That at the time of making such subscription, the sum of Fifteen thousand Dollars ($15,000) was paid in in cash, the prescribed percentage, to wit : five per cent of the par value of the stock so subscribed for, and that the said books of subscription were thereupon closed.

Thereafter, and on the 14th day of June, 1888, notices were served on the persons who had subscribed to the said Articles of Association and form of subscription, whereby a meeting of said subscribers was, by said Commissioners, duly called to be held at the office of said Commissioners, on June 28th, 1888, at Room No. 6, Hall of Records, in the City of Brooklyn, at ten o'clock in the forenoon, a copy of which notice and proof of service thereof is hereto annexed.

On the same day this Board duly appointed Edward Murphy and Charles N. McGuire, as Inspectors of Election at said meeting. That said Inspectors thereupon duly qualified in form shown by the copies of their affidavit and the certificate of the Notary Public hereto annexed.

That on the 26th day of June, 1888, the said meeting was held, at which the following persons were duly elected as Directiors of the said Fulton Elevated Railway Company, viz:

 James Jourdan, Wendell Goodwin,
 James O. Sheldon, Henry J. Robinson,
 Harvey Farrington, James H. Frothingham,
 S. Newton Smith, Henry J. Davison,
   Edward A. Abbot.

That the proceedings of the said Inspectors and of the said meeting appear in and by the copy of the certificate of the said Inspectors, which is hereto annexed. Each of the papers hereto annexed has been signed by Thomas S. Moore, one of the undersigned.

In witness whereof we have hereunto set our hands this 2d of July, 1888.

   THOMAS S. MOORE,
   GEORGE W. ALMY,
   GEORGE W. BROWN,
   THOMAS H. MCGRATH,
   EUGENE DOHERTY.

STATE OF NEW YORK, } ss.:
County of Kings, }

Before me, Edgar M. Cullen, a Justice of the Supreme Court, this 2d day of July, 1888, appeared Thomas S. Moore, George W. Almy, George W. Brown, Thomas H. McGrath and Eugene Doherty, to me personally known, and known to me to be the five Commissioners appointed in February, 1888, by the Mayor of the City of Brooklyn, under Chapter 606 of the Laws of the State of New York, and the act or acts amendatory thereof, passed June 18, 1875, and each of them being by me duly sworn, did depose and say under oath: That he has read the foregoing certificate by him and the other Commissioners subscribed, within the papers therein referred to, and thereto annexed, and that the matters therein stated are true.

Sworn to before me, this }
2d day of July, 1888. }

   EDGAR M. CULLEN,
     J. S. C.

The following papers were annexed to the Certificate of the Commissioners, which papers are not here set forth as they already appear in these minutes:

Articles of Association, which appear on pages 140 to 167 of the Minutes, both inclusive.

Book of Subscription, consisting of said Articles of Association, together with Form of Subscription on pages 170 and 171 of the Minutes, the Articles of Association and Form of Subscription each being subscribed by the persons named, and in the manner set forth on pages 178, 178a and 178b of the Minutes.

Copies of the Powers of Attorney to subscribe to the capital stock of the Fulton Elevated Railway Company, being twenty in number, in the form recorded on pages 179 and 180 of the Minutes.

Notice of Meeting for Organization, with Proof of Service of same, on pages 186, 187 and 188 of the Minutes.

Oaths of Inspectors of Election, on page 189 of the Minutes.

Certificate of Inspectors of Election, on pages 191 and 192 of the Minutes.

On motion of Commissioner Almy, the compensation of the Stenographer was fixed at $750 and disbursements.

The following letter was received and ordered to be entered in full on the minutes:

FULTON ELEVATED RAILWAY COMPANY,

Brooklyn, July 2, 1888.

GEORGE W. ALMY, Esq.,
    Treasurer of the Rapid Transit Commission.
Dear Sir:

You are hereby authorized and empowered to pay to each of the Commissioners fifteen hundred dollars as a compensation for his services as Commissioner.

    (Signed)   Truly yours,

JAMES JOURDAN,
President.

On motion it was ressolved, that the Treasurer be authorized to pay each Commissioner $1500, and Mrs. E. F. Pettengill $750.

Adjourned to Friday, July 6, 1888, at 9.30 A. M.

GEORGE W. BROWN,
Secretary.

COMMISSIONERS OF RAPID TRANSIT,
City of Brooklyn,
Room No. 6, Hall of Records,
Friday, July 6, 1888, 9.30 A. M.

Present—George W. Brown and Eugene Doherty.

There being no quorum present, the meeting adjourned to Monday, July 9th, 1888, at 9.30 A. M.

GEORGE W. BROWN,
Secretary.

COMMISSIONERS OF RAPID TRANSIT,
City of Brooklyn,
Room No. 6, Hall of Records,
Monday, July 9, 1888, 9.30 A. M.

Present—Commissioners George W. Almy, George W. Brown, Thomas H. McGrath and Eugene Doherty.

Commissioner McGrath was elected temporary Chairman.

The minutes of the meetings of the 2d and 6th insts. were read and approved.

The Secretary reported that he had delivered the Commissioner's certificate, setting forth the Articles of Association heretofore prepared by this Board, and the organization of the Fulton Elevated Railway Company, to the Directors of that Company.

The Board adjourned subject to the call of the President.

GEORGE W. BROWN,
Secretary.

COMMISSIONERS OF RAPID TRANSIT,
City of Brooklyn,
Room No. 6, Hall of Records,
Thursday, July 19, 1888, 9.30 A. M.

Present—Commissioners Thomas S. Moore, George W. Almy and Eugene Doherty.

The minutes of the meeting of the 9th inst. were read and approved.

A bill from Mrs. Pettengill for disbursements, amounting to $133.33 was read, approved, and the Treasurer was ordered to pay the same.

The Treasurer reported that he had paid the following bills:

Charles N. McGuire, Inspector, . . $	10.00
Edward Murphy, Inspector, . .	10.00
Thomas S. Moore, Disbursements, .	24.89
The World, Advertising, . .	132.40
The Standard-Union, Advertising, .	10.50
The Brooklyn Daily Times, . .	118.44
The Brooklyn Citizen, ...	153.15
Henry Hamilton, Stage, . . .	10.00
Samuel R. Probasco, Engineer, . .	750.00
Thomas S. Moore, ...	1,500.00

George W. Almy,	1,500.00
George W. Brown,	1,500.00
Thomas H. McGrath,	1,500.00
Eugene Doherty,	1,500 00
The *Brooklyn Daily Eagle*, Advertising,	145.20
George W. Brown, Disbursements,	12.00
Mortimer B. O'Shea, Janitor,	50.00
The *Brooklyn Freie Presse*, Advertising,	75.00
E. F. Pettengill. Assistant Secretary,	750.00
E. F. Pettengill, Disbursements,	133.33
	$10,259.91

The Board adjourned subject to the call of the President.

GEORGE W. BROWN,

Secretary.

COMMISSIONERS OF RAPID TRANSIT,
City of Brooklyn,
Room No. 6. Hall of Records,
Tuesday, August 7, 1888, 9.30 A. M.

The Board met pursuant to the call of the President.

Present—Commissioners Thomas S. Moore, George W. Almy, George W. Brown, Thomas H. McGrath and Eugene Doherty.

Minutes of the meeting of July 19th were read and approved.

The Secretary reported that the proof of the printed minutes would be ready on the 8th inst.

On motion of Commissioner Doherty the Treasurer was authorized to pay the bill of the *Standard-Union*, for advertising, amounting to $82.00.

On motion of Commissioner McGrath the Treasurer was authorized to pay the *Brooklyn Citizen* bill for printing minutes, when work is completed according to contract.

Adjourned to meet at office of the President, 102 Broadway, New York, at 12 o'clock M., Friday, August 10th.

GEORGE W. BROWN,
Secretary.

COMMISSIONERS OF RAPID TRANSIT,
City of Brooklyn.

Friday, August 10, 1888, 12 M.

The Board met pursuant to adjournment, at the office of the President, 102 Broadway, New York.

Present—Commissioners Thomas S. Moore, George W. Almy, George W. Brown and Eugene Doherty.

Minutes of the meeting of the 7th inst. were read and approved.

The Treasurer reported the payment of the *Standard-Union* bill for advertising, amounting to $82.00.

On motion of Commissioner Doherty it was

Resolved, That the Secretary of this Board be and hereby is authorized and directed to deliver to the Fulton Elevated Railway Company all plans, specifications, drawings, maps, books and papers in the possession of this Board.

On motion of Commissioner Doherty,

Resolved, The Treasurer of this Commission be and hereby is directed to pay to James H. Frothingham, Treasurer of the Fulton Elevated Railway Company, all monies remaining in the Long Island Loan and Trust Company, to the credit of George W. Almy, Treasurer of this Commission, after deducting the expenses incurred by this Commission and amounts paid the said Commissioners for their salaries.

On motion of Commissioner Doherty,

Resolved, That the Secretary be and is hereby directed to verify the minutes of this Board of Commissioners and deliver the said minutes to the Secretary of the Fulton Elevated Railway Company.

On motion of Commissioner Doherty,

Resolved, That the Secretary be and is hereby directed to verify a copy of the minutes of this Board of Commissioners and deliver the same to the Mayor of the City of Brooklyn.

On motion, adjourned to Monday, August 13th, at 3 P.M.

GEORGE W. BROWN,
Secretary.

COMMISSIONERS OF RAPID TRANSIT,
City of Brooklyn,
Room No. 6, Hall of Records,
Monday, August 13th, 1888, 3 P. M.

Board met pursuant to adjournment.

Present—Commissioners George W. Almy, George W. Brown, and Eugene Doherty.

Commissioner Almy was elected Chairman, *pro tem.*

Minutes of the meeting of August 10th, read and approved.

The Secretary not being ready to close the minutes, adjourned to August 16th, at 3 P. M. at the office of the Treasurer, No. 42 Park Place, New York.

GEORGE W. BROWN,
Secretary.

COMMISSIONERS OF RAPID TRANSIT,

City of Brooklyn,

Room No. 6, Hall of Records,

Thursday, August 16th, 1888, 3 P. M.

Board met at 42 Park Place, N. Y., pursuant to adjournment.

A quorum not being present, adjourned subject to the call of the Secretary.

GEORGE G. BROWN,
Secretary.

COMMISSIONERS OF RAPID TRANSIT,
City of Brooklyn,
416 Bedford Ave.,
Friday, August 24th, 3 P.M.

The Board met pursuant to call of the Secretary.

Commissioner Almy was elected Chairman *pro tem.*

A quorum being present, the minutes of the meetings of August 13th and 16th were read and approved.

The Secretary reported that he had delivered to Mr. Henry J. Robinson, Secretary of the Fulton Elevated Railway Co., the minutes and all other books, papers and plans, as instructed by resolution of the Board passed August 10th.

The Treasurer reported having paid *The Brooklyn Citizen* bill for printing minutes and proceedings of the Board, amounting to $296.50, also that he had paid to James H. Frothingham, Treasurer of the The Fulton Elevated Railway Co., $4,361.59, balance remaining in his hands, after payment of all bills and expenses of the Board.

There being no further business to come before this Board, on motion of Commissioner Brown, the Board adjourned.

GEORGE W. BROWN,
Secretary.

Printed in Dunstable, United Kingdom